TOASTS

Early Toasting Image. A mid-19th-century ambrotype of two gents celebrating for the camera. *(Author's collection)*

Books by Paul Dickson

THINK TANKS

THE GREAT AMERICAN ICE CREAM BOOK

THE FUTURE OF THE WORKPLACE

THE ELECTRONIC BATTLEFIELD

THE MATURE PERSON'S GUIDE TO KITES,
YO-YOS, FRISBEES AND OTHER CHILDLIKE
DIVERSIONS

OUT OF THIS WORLD:
AMERICAN SPACE PHOTOGRAPHY

THE FUTURE FILE

CHOW: A COOK'S TOUR OF MILITARY FOOD

THE OFFICIAL RULES

THE OFFICIAL EXPLANATIONS

TOASTS

Paul Dickson

TOASTS

The Complete Book of the
Best Toasts, Sentiments, Blessings,
Curses, and Graces

A Dell Trade Paperback

A DELL TRADE PAPERBACK BOOK

Published by
Dell Publishing Co., Inc.
1 Dag Hammarskjold Plaza
New York, New York 10017

Dell ® TM 681510, Dell Publishing Co., Inc.

ISBN: 0-440-58741-7

Reprinted by arrangement with Delacorte Press
Printed in the United States of America
First Dell Trade Paperback Printing—October 1982

CONTENTS

INTRODUCTION

There are a number of old things that we are well rid of—child labor, scurvy, glass shampoo bottles, and too many others to mention—but there are still others that we are foolish to let slip away. Toasting is one of them.

A toast is a basic form of human expression that can be used for virtually any emotion from love to rage (although raging toasts tend to cross the line into the realm of curses). They can be sentimental, cynical, lyric, comic, defiant, long, short, or a single word. The names and traditions associated with the custom are many and date back to the ancient world. They are also very much a part of our literary heritage, and with the exception of the last few decades, there has not been a writer of note from Milton to Mencken who has not left us at least one good toast. What's more, some of our favorite fictional characters have uttered classics—among them, Tiny Tim's "God bless us every one!" from *A Christmas Carol* and Rick's "Here's lookin' at you, kid!" from *Casablanca.* Most important, however, is that they are so useful. They are a medium through which such deep feelings as love, hope, high spirits, and admiration can be quickly, conveniently, and sincerely expressed.

There was a time, not that long ago, when one could not go to a luncheon—let alone a banquet or a wedding —without hearing a series of carefully proposed and executed toasts. Toasts were the test of one's ability to come up with an appropriate inspiration to sip to the honor of some person, sentiment, or institution. It really didn't matter if it was an original written for the occasion or a time-tested classic passed down from Elizabethan times. What was important was whether or not the toast worked to keep the proceedings moving at a jolly pace.

About a third of the way into this century, however, the custom of creative, thoughtful toasting began to erode. It seemed as if people had less time and inclination to work them up or memorize them. Nor was this decline limited to the United States. British author John Pudney wrote in 1963 of "decline in the eloquence and variety of the toast in the English language. The last two generations at least seem to find themselves embarrassed by the formality of toasting."

In recent years, the decline has continued to the point at which a set of wedding toasts may have no more style, grace, or imagination than a hastily yelped, "Here's to the bride and groom! Here's to Fred and Maxine!" Moreover, most of our workaday toasts still in use are of the quick, down-the-hatch variety in which the custom has been reduced to a mumbled word (Cheers!—Prosit!) or phrase (Happy days!—Down the hatch!—Hair on your chest!) uttered from habit rather than any real sentiment.

Ironically, some of the better old toasts have devolved to the level where they are virtually meaningless either because they have been shortened or lost their original context. The ubiquitous "Here's mud in your eye!" is a good case in point. A fuller, much older version ends the line with ". . . while I look over your lovely sweetheart!" "Mud in your eye" had an entirely different context in the days when the American West was opening up. A pioneering farmer about to leave the East would stop in the local tavern to say good-bye to friends, who would toast mud in his eyes. In this situation those proposing the toast were hoping the farmer would find soft, rich, and damp soil that would be thrown up as specks of mud as the farmer ploughed it.

Toasting is still an important custom on such high and formal occasions as state dinners and diplomatic receptions. Yet in this realm, a different kind of erosion has taken place. Official toasts—which have always tended to be light, friendly, and anecdotal—have become political vehicles in recent years. Increasingly, they are long, windy, political addresses.

Things began to sour in 1975 when Zambian President Kenneth Kuanda startled the guests at a White House dinner when he responded to a traditional toast from President Ford with a twenty-minute "toast," which in reality was a statement of his nation's foreign policy. In 1978, the late Marshal Josip Broz Tito bested Kuanda with a rambling forty-minute dissertation on the international political scene. Since then the forty-five-minute barrier has fallen, and there is a distinct possibility that by the time you read this the one-hour toast will be commonplace.

Not only is conviviality missing from these "toasts," but some are downright hostile. In early 1979, when President Carter and Mexican President López Portillo traded a well-publicized set of diplomatic insults in Mexico City, they called their attacks toasts. That exchange began as Portillo ingraciously led with a wide-ranging indictment of the United States, and a dazed Carter jabbed back with a tasteless recollection of a bout of Montezuma's Revenge.

A more recent development introduced by President Carter has been to actually include a question and answer session as part of his toast.

Sad to say, there is not one consistently good pocket of toasting left in the United States, not even among those who study the many periods when toasting was more than a murmured "Bottoms up!" Not long ago there was a story in *The Washington Post* that told of a distinguished Elizabethan scholar proposing two toasts, to Shakespeare and one of his characters. In their entirety, the toasts: "To Falstaff" and "To the Bard." This display becomes even more appalling with the realization that Shakespeare's plays contain scores of toasts

White House Toast. President Carter toasts Ireland's Prime Minister John M. Lynch and Mrs. Lynch, November 1979. *(White House Photograph)*

and lines that have been used as toasts for hundreds of years.

Enough. The point is made that we have all but abandoned a useful medium and form of communication in an age of media and communication. Simply stated, the purpose of this book is to be the vehicle for a massive revival.

If this seems a bit much, consider the fact that we are in the midst of a period of deep revival that has already witnessed the return of roller skates, quilts, ice cream parlors, wood-burning stoves, backgammon, canning and preserving, bib overalls, magic shows, midwifery, burlesque, juggling, mineral water, vegetable gardens, zucchini, windmills, candles, kites, gnomes, rural migration, sensible woolens, the L. L. Bean style, cowboy garb, joke telling, and more.

Here's to it!

A BRIEF HISTORY OF RAISED GLASSES

The custom of drinking a "health" to the prosperity, happiness, luck, or good health of another dates back into antiquity—and, perhaps, into prehistory.

It is impossible to point to the moment when the first rude vessel was raised in honor of an ancient god or to the health of a newborn baby. Nor do we have any idea when a parched traveler lifted his cup in thanks to the man or woman who gave him wine.

What we do know is that the custom of drinking to health permeated the ancient world. Ulysses drank to the health of Achilles in the "Odyssey." An early Greek custom called for a pledge of three cups—one to Mercury, one to the Graces, and one to Zeus. In Rome, drinking to another's health became so important, the Senate decreed that all diners must drink to Augustus at every meal. Fabius Maximus declared that no man should eat or drink before he had prayed for him and drank to his health.

The ancient Hebrews, Persians, and Egyptians were toasters as were the Saxons, Huns, and other tribes. For instance, in *The Decline and Fall of the Roman Empire,* Edward Gibbon tells of a feast among the Huns at which their leader Attila led no less than three rounds of healths for each course during a long dinner of many courses.

Over time the simple act of toasting another became embellished and intertwined with other customs. (It would not be until the seventeenth century that the act was actually referred to as a toast. More on that shortly.) At some point along the way, for instance, the gesture of clinking glasses or cups became popular. It has been long believed that this began during the Christian era, as the original intention of the clink was to produce a bell-like noise so as to banish the devil, who is repelled by bells. Another legendary explanation for glass clinking is that all five senses should come into play to get the greatest pleasure from a drink. It is tasted, touched, seen, smelled, and—with the clink—heard.

An odd but essential custom was added to British tippling during the invasion by the Danes during the tenth century. This was the custom of pledging another's health in the most literal terms—that is, a friend stating his intention of guarding the drinker from harm while he tosses back a drink. This stemmed from the objectionable Danish habit of cutting the throats of Englishmen while they were drinking. Shakespeare's line from *Timon of Athens,* "Great men should drink with harness on their throats," is one of several old literary references to this murderous behavior.

Still another morbidly fascinating custom from Northern Europe is that of drinking mead or ale from the skull of a fallen enemy. The Scots and Scandinavians both practiced this primitive form of recycling, and the Highland Scotch *skiel* (tub) and the Norse *skoal* (bowl) derive from it. The modern toast, *skoal,* in turn comes from the Old Norse term. This custom persisted through the eleventh century, after which only an occasional skull was converted into a drinking vessel. Lord Byron acquired a human skull, had it mounted as a drinking vessel, and wrote an inscription for it that read:

Start not, nor deem my spirit fled:
In me behold the only skull

From which, unlike a living head,
Whatever flows is never dull.

I lived, I loved, I quaff'd like thee:
I died: let earth my bones resign:
Fill up—thou canst not injure me,
The worm hath fouler lips than thine.

Better to hold the sparkling grape,
Than nurse the earthworm's slimy brood;
And circle in the goblet's shape
The drink of gods, than reptile's food.

Where once my wit, perchance, hath shone,
In aid of others let me shine;
And when, alas! our brains are gone,
What nobler substitute than wine?

Quaff while thou canst, another race
When thou and thine, like me, are sped,
May rescue thee from earth's embrace,
And rhyme and revel with the dead.

The first *recorded* instance of a toast being offered in England occurred in 450 A.D. at a great feast given by the British King Vortigern to his Saxon allies. Rowena, the beautiful daughter of the Saxon leader Hengist, held up a large goblet filled with a spiced drink and drank to the king, saying, *"Louerd King, waes hael!"*— "Lord King, be of health!"—to which he replied, *"Drink, hael!"*

According to the account of medieval historian Geoffery of Monmouth, the festivity did not stop there. Vortigern kissed Rowena and then made passionate love to her. Intoxicated, he then bargained with Hengist for her hand. A deal was struck by which Hengist got the province of Kent in exchange for Rowena. Vortigern and Rowena were married that evening.

For at least a thousand years drinking in Britain was commonly accompanied by the same verbal exchange, although *waes hael* became *wassail*. One of the earliest known Christmas carols, dating from the days of the Norman minstrels, ends with these lines:

Each must drain his cup of wine,

And I the first will toss off mine:
Thus I advise,
Here then I bid you all *Wassail,*
Cursed be he who will not say *Drink hail.*

Over the years the term "wassail" became associated with Christmas and the New Year, the times of the greatest festivity, and by the seventeenth century the meaning had narrowed to the specific one of drinking from a large bowl or loving cup on Christmas Day and Twelfth Night. While people of means prepared their own wassail, groups of poor people commonly went from door to door with an empty bowl, which they expected to be filled at every stop. Some prefaced their request with a medley of Christmas carols while others chanted something more threatening:

Come, butler, come fill us a bowl of the best;
Then we hope that your soul in heaven may
    rest;
But if you draw us a bowl of the small,
Then down shall go butler, bowl and all.

Anglo-Saxon Dinner Party. Picture from a 10th-century manuscript showing feasting and health drinking.

A variation of this custom was for a group to go door to door with a beverage of their own making for which they would expect to be dearly paid. There were songs for this as well:

> Good dame, here at your door
> Our wassail we begin,
> We are all maidens poor,
> We now pray let us in,
> With our wassail.

Some of the old wassailing songs were little more than toasts set to music:

> Here's to _____ and his right ear,
> God send our maister a Happy New Year;
> A Happy New Year as e'er he did see—
> With my wassailing bowl I drink to thee.

> Here's to _____ and her right eye,
> God send our mistress a good Christmas pie:
> A good Christmas pie as e'er I did see—
> With my wassailing bowl I drink to thee.

The present custom of caroling from door to door derives from all of this.

Although people had been drinking to one another for centuries, the actual term "toast" did not come along until the late seventeenth century, when it was the custom to place a piece of toast or crouton in a drink. This is alluded to in many drinking songs and ditties of the period including this one published in 1684:

> A toast is like a sot; or what is most
> Compatitive, a sot is like a toast;
> For when their substance is liquor sink,
> Both properly are said to be in drink.

The exact reason for doing this has been blurred by time, but various hints point to the conclusion that it was either believed to improve the flavor of the drink in the manner of a spice, or that it was a built-in snack, a bit of token nourishment. Whatever the reason, the practice was common, and virtually anything found floating in a drink was referred to as "toast."

The name change occurred during the days of Charles II (1660–1684) in the resort city of Bath, where many went for the ardent spirits and warm mineral baths. The exact moment of the name change was recorded in 1709 in *The Tatler* by Issac Bickerstaffe:

> It happened that on a publick day a celebrated beauty of those times was in the Cross Bath, and one of the crowd of her admirers took a glass of the water in which the fair one stood and drank her health to the company. There was in the place a gay fellow, half fuddled, who offered to jump in, and swore though he liked not the liquor, he would have the toast. He was opposed in his resolution; yet this whim gave foundation to the present honour which is done to the lady we mention in our liquor, who has ever since been called a toast.[*]

Toasting became immensely popular during the seventeenth century. This was especially true in the British Isles. "To drink at table," wrote one Englishman, "without drinking to the health of some one special, would be considered drinking on the sly, and as an act of incivility."

Popularity bred excess. The English discovered the Scandinavian custom of not only drinking to everyone present, but to all of one's *absent* friends as well. Suddenly, one did not have to limit oneself to the mere twenty drinks normally pledged at a party of twenty.

Each nation had its own customs—almost always excessive. In Scotland, for instance, it was the custom to drink sparingly during the meal, allow the women to withdraw to the drawing room, and then bring in a large punch bowl filled with whiskey, hot water, and sugar. Goblets or mugs were used, and each round re-

---

[*] *The Tatler,* Vol. 1., No. 24.

quired a toast, a quick drink, and a turned-over vessel to prove that all had been drunk. One scholar of the period wrote, "During the seventeenth and the earlier portion of the eighteenth century, after-dinner drinking was protracted for eight to ten hours."

On important occasions, the toaster mounted his chair, placed his right foot on the table, and bellowed out a favorite sentiment—"May ne'er waur be amang us," "May the pleasures of the evening bear the reflection of the morning," or whatever. All of this was accompanied by lusty cheering.

The toasting and hoisting that accompanied Scotch weddings were enough to put a cramp in the arm. According to an account from 1682 the process began when the parents of the bride and groom met to make the wedding arrangements. The two families would meet at a point equidistant between their two homes and if all went well, they would bring out an agreement bottle of whiskey with which the coming wedding would be toasted. Closer to the actual event was the predecessor of today's bachelor party. The male friends of the bride and the male friends of the groom would meet halfway between the bride's and groom's houses. Each group would appoint a "champion" and the two men would race, either on horseback or foot, to the bride's house where the winner would receive a beribboned bottle. The bottle would be brought back to be passed among the assembled men as they drank to the bride's health. Then came the wedding and more toasting and drinking.

This period also witnessed some strange toasting customs. One practice called for men to show their affection for a woman by stabbing themselves in the arm, mixing their blood in their wine, and drinking to the lady in question. The Prince of Morocco in Shakespeare's *The Merchant of Venice* alludes to this when he talks of making ". . . an incision for your love," and a song of the time rightly proclaimed:

> I stabbed my arm to drink her health,
> The more fool I, the more fool I.

No less repulsive was the custom, prevalent among

THE VINTAGE.

"The Vintage." Stipple etching by Italian artist Francesco Bartolozzi (c. 1725–1815). *(The Christian Brothers Collection at the Wine Museum of San Francisco)*

students of the period, of proving one's love by toasting in imaginative but progressively nauseous concoctions. In his *History of Toasting,* Richard Valpy French tells of two Oxford students grossly proving their devotion to a beauty named Molly: "One, determined to prove that his love did not stick at trifles, took a spoonful of soot, mixed it with his wine, and drank off the mixture. His companion, determined not to be outdone, brought from his closet a phial of ink, which he drank, exclaiming, 'To triumph and Miss Molly.' "

As if this were not enough, student innovators of the time also first hit upon the wretched business of grabbing a woman's shoe, using it to ladle wine from a common bowl, and toasting the shoe's owner. Neither the shoe nor the wine benefited.

Though this was not a time of great subtlety, there was an occasional hint of it. The outlawed Jacobites would publicly, though secretly, drink to their exiled Stuart monarch, Bonnie Prince Charlie, by passing their glass over a bowl of water. Thus, while ostensibly toasting the Hanoverian King George II, they were actually drinking to "the king across the water."

Less subtle was this Jacobite toast:

God bless the King, I mean the Faith's
  Defender,
God bless—no harm in blessing—the Pretender,
But which is Pretender, and which is King?
God bless us all! that's quite another thing.

If anything, it appears that toasting became even more pervasive during the boozy eighteenth and early nineteenth centuries. New institutions emerged, most notably the position of toastmaster. In Henry Fielding's *Tom Jones*, published in 1749, there is reference to a toastmaster whose duties were to propose and announce toasts. In those days the duties of the toastmaster tended to be refereelike in that his main function was to give all toasters a fair chance to make their contribution. Then, as now, the prime rule of toastmastering was to keep sober and offend nobody.

For the most part, the toasts of this period tended to be short, crisp, and to the point—or as one student of toasting has put it, ". . . these were not an excuse for speeches but for wit and wine." A case in point were the toasts that were given in the officer's wardroom during the days when Horatio Nelson commanded the English navy. The first toast would always be to the king with the second (changing each day) prescribed as follows:

> MONDAY: "Our ships at sea."
> TUESDAY: "Our men."
> WEDNESDAY: "Ourselves."
> THURSDAY: "A bloody war or a sickly season."
> FRIDAY: "A willing foe and sea room."
> SATURDAY: "Sweethearts and wives."
> SUNDAY: "Absent friends."

In contrast, the toasts of the era's sailors were more poetic:

> The wind that blows, the ship that goes
> And the lass that loves a sailor.
>
> Damn his eyes,
> If he ever tries
> To rob a poor man of his ale.

If the toasts were frugal, the drinking that went with them was anything but. In Dyott's *Diary 1781–1845* an account is given of a dinner at which the Prince Regent, afterward George IV, was one of the celebrants:

> The Prince took the chair himself and ordered me to be his Vice. We had a very good dinner and he sent wine of his own, the very best Claret I ever tasted. We had the Grenadiers drawn up in front of the mess-room windows to fire a volley in honour of the toasts. As soon as dinner was over he began. He did not drink himself: he always drinks Madeira. He took very good care to see everybody fill, and he gave 23 bumpers without a halt. In the course of my experience I never saw such fair drinking. When he had finished his list of bumpers, I begged leave as Vice to give the Superior, and recommended it to the Society to stand up on our

chairs with three times three, taking their time
from the Vice. I think it was the most laughable
sight I ever beheld to see our Governor, our General, and the Commodore all so drunk they could
scarce stand on the floor, hoisted up on their chairs
with each a bumper in his hand; and the three
times three cheers was what they were afraid to
attempt for fear of falling. I then proposed his
Royal Highness and a good wind whenever he
sailed (he intended sailing on Monday) with the
same ceremony. He stood at the head of the table
during both these toasts, and I never saw a man
laugh so in my life. When we had drunk the last,
the old Governor desired to know if we had any
more as he said if once he got down he should
never get up again. His Royal Highness saw we
were all pretty well done, and he walked off. There
were twenty dined, we drank sixty-three bottles of
wine.

There is ample evidence to suggest that such excess
was as common in America. One account from New
York in 1770 describes a dinner held for a Captain
McDougal and forty-four of his friends. They used
forty-five pounds of steak and drank forty-five toasts.
A description of a New York dinner in 1787 tells of the
diners toasting their way through fifteen kinds of wine
and two beers.

In fact, nobody seemed to have a lock on such behavior. A custom that became popular in Edinburgh in
the nineteenth century was known as "saving the ladies." Lord Cockburn described the custom in his *Jour-
nals:*

> When after any fashionable assembly the male
> guests had conducted their fair partners to their
> homes, they returned to the supper-room. Then
> one of the number would drink to the health of the
> lady he professed to admire, and in so doing empty
> his glass. Another gentleman would name another
> lady, also drinking a bumper in her honour. The
> former would reply by swallowing a social glass to

his lady, followed by the other, each combatant persisting till one of the two fell upon the floor. Other couples followed in like fashion. These drinking competitions were regarded with interest by gentlewomen who next morning enquired as to the prowess of their champions.

Cockburn, by the way, was literally horrified by the inane and sentimental lines that his contemporaries would utter as "an excuse for the glass." Some of the toasts that most disgusted him were: "May the hand of charity wipe away the tears from the eyes of sorrow," "May the pleasure of the evening bear the reflection of the morning," and, saving the worst for last, "The reflection of the moon in the cawn bosom of the lake."

Over the years such excesses prompted more than a few decrees, rulings, and antitoast crusades. This opposition is worthy of a moment's digression.

Among others, Charles the Great, Maximilian, and Charles V enacted laws against the vice. Even Louis XIV, not one to be put off by a touch of debauchery, finally forbade the offering of toasts at his court. It is noteworthy that one of the main objectives of the first known temperance society (founded in 1517) was the abolition of the custom of toasting. In the American Colonies, a law was put into effect in Massachusetts in 1634 that banned the custom of drinking to another's health, a practice that was deemed an "abominable . . . useless ceremony." (The law, largely ignored, was repealed in 1645.) In England a small legion of moralists, politicians, and religious leaders opposed toasting and its attendant evils. In 1713, for instance, the Bishop of Cork became so upset with the practice of drinking to the dead that he issued both a stern injunction and a widely-distributed pamphlet against it. Typical of the attacks on the custom was this injection from Lord Chief Justice Sir Matthew Hale, which was written for his grandchildren:

I will not have you begin, or pledge any health, for it is become one of the greatest artifices of drinking

LE VIN.

"Le Vin." Lithograph by L. Scherer of Germany (1827–1876). *(The Christian Brothers Collection at the Wine Museum of San Francisco)*

and occasions of quarrelling in the Kingdom. If you pledge another, and a third, and so onward; and if you pledge as many as will be drank, you must be debauched and drunk. If they will needs know the reason for your refusal, it is fair to answer: "That your grandfather who brought you up, from whom, under God, you have the estate you enjoy or expect, left this in command with you, that you should never begin or pledge a health."

Of all those who crusaded against toasting, however, it would be hard to find one with a greater antagonism than William Prynne who, among other things, devoted a whole book to the link between the devil and the custom. The book, *Health's Sicknesse,* was published in 1628 and alleges ". . . the great, Deuill-god Jupiter was the first inventer, founder, and instituter of our Hellish and Heathenish Healthes." At another point he asserts ". . . that this drinking and quaffing of healthes had its origin and birth from Pagans, heathens, and infidels, yea, from the very Deuill himself; that it is but a worldly, carnall, prophane, nay, heathenish and deuillish custom, which sauors of nothing else but Paganisme . . ."

Prynne was certainly true to his convictions and not one to backslide at a party. On June 6, 1664, Samuel Pepys attended a dinner at which Prynne ". . . would not drink any health, no, not the King's but sat down with his hat on all the while; but nobody took notice of him at all."

Interestingly, Prynne is hardly alone in his antitoast writing. Ranging from St. Augustine ("This filthy and unhappy custom of drinking healths . . .") up through the beginning of this century, a great body of literature has been amassed against the custom. In fact, the most thorough book written on the subject, *The History of Toasting* by the Rev. Richard Valpy French, is written by a man who despised toasting. Though scrupulously factual, French delights in bringing to light gruesome, bloody episodes in which toasting took place. He outdoes himself in telling us of an ancient Danish ballad:

> In one very old one, a husband after treacherously murdering his wife's twelve brothers during their sleep, and whilst they were his guests, fills a cup with their blood, which he brings to his wife that she might pledge him in it. Many years after, the wife, in retaliation, whilst her husband's relations are visiting him, steals out of bed at dead of night, murders them all, fills a cup with their gore, returns to her husband's chamber, and whilst he still sleeps securely, ties him hand and foot. She then wakes him, and after mockingly asking him to pledge her in the cup of blood, dispatches him. At

that moment their baby in its cradle wakes up and cries out, so the mother, fearing lest in afterlife her son should avenge his father's murder, makes matters safe by quietly dashing its brains out.

French also uncovered such things as an ancient tribe, "the old Guebres," who exposed the corpses of their parents to the "fowls of the air," then reserved only the skulls from the decay and fashioned cups from them.

Such skulduggery notwithstanding, there were those who promoted toasting as a blessing, as an amenity and a graceful custom with, as one Victorian writer put it, ". . . a quality as pleasant as a handshake, as warm as a kiss."

An early—if not the earliest—book entirely devoted to toasts and toasting is J. Roach's *The Royal Toastmaster,* published in London in 1791. Roach was clearly intent on cleaning up the image of the custom. "Its use," he says of the toast, "is well known to all ranks, as a stimulative to hilarity, and an incentive to innocent mirth, to loyal truth, to pure morality and to mutual affection." At one point he ascribes great power to it:

> A Toast or Sentiment very frequently excites good humour, and revives languid conversation; often does it, when properly applied, cool the heat of resentment, and blunt the edge of animosity. A well-applied Toast is acknowledged, universally, to sooth the flame of acrimony, when season and reason oft used their efforts to no purpose.

Roach laments "former times" and to some extent the "contemporary custom" of banning women from toasting sessions. In introducing his book of "decent toasts" he points out that the reason women are often excluded is the indecency of many toasts and general climate of "boisterous and illiberal mirth."

If nothing else, Roach did help set a new tone. His toasts were predictably proper ("Confusion to the minions of vice!" and "May reason be the pilot when passion blows the gale!") and politically liberal in the

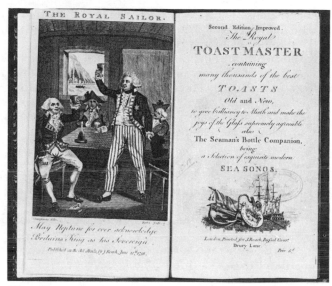

"The Royal Toastmaster." Frontispiece and title page from Roach's 1791 collection. *(Rare book collection, Library of Congress)*

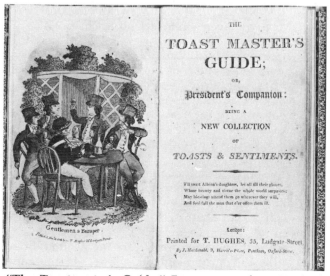

"The Toastmaster's Guide." Front matter from Hughes's collection of 1806. *(Rare book collection, Library of Congress)*

modern sense ("To the abolition of the slave trade!"; "The rights of man!"; and, incredibly for 1791 England, "The liberty of North America!")

Another early collection of toasts was *The Toastmaster's Guide* by T. Hughes, which was published in London in 1806. Like Roach, Hughes's favored the quick one-liner of the time; but unlike Roach, he was not above a little early-nineteenth-century spice with his toasts. A sampling from Hughes's collection:

> The two that makes a third.
> The rose of pleasure without the thorn.
> The modest maid, who covered herself with her lover.
> The commodity most thought of and least talk'd of.
> Mirth, wine and love.
> May the works of our nights never fear the day-light.
> Old wine and young women.
> Prudence and temperance with claret and champagne.
> Love without fear, and life without care.
> May we never want a friend to cheer us, or a bottle to cheer him.
> A generous heart and a miser's fortune.
> Short shoes and long corns to the enemies of Great Britain.
> May we do as we would be done by.
> May we live in pleasure and die out of debt.
> A blush of detection to the lovers of deceit.
> May British cuckolds never want horns.

Many short toasts that are still heard today—"Good luck until we are tired of it!"; "May poverty be a day's march behind us!"; "Champagne to our real friends and real pain to our sham friends!"—appear in Hughes's book.

Toasting transferred easily to the United States, where the Revolution and the newness of the nation were great inspirations. During the war the toasts tended in the direction of curses:

To the enemies of our country! May they have cobweb breeches, a porcupine saddle, a hard-trotting horse, and an eternal journey.

After the war no official dinner or celebration was complete without thirteen toasts, one for each state. For many years, the thirteen toasts were obligatory at local Fourth of July celebrations. At such times each toast was followed by an artillery salute, three cheers from the crowd, and a song.

Although the exact toasts differed somewhat from locale to locale, they were generally always patriotic, proud, and nonpartisan. They were dedicated to things ranging from the holiday itself ("May it ever be held in grateful remembrance by the American people") to the nation's former presidents ("In the evenings of well-spent lives pleased with the fruits of their labors, they cheerfully await the summons that shall waft them to brighter abodes.") Invariably, there was a toast to the signers of the Declaration of Independence:

From this act of treason against the British Crown sprang a chart of Liberty and Emancipation broad as the universe and filled with glad tiding and good will towards men. They who perilled their lives by this noble act will live and be cherished in the hearts of free men.

The origin of the thirteen toasts appears to date from the series of banquets held in honor of George Washington on his retirement. At one such banquet in Annapolis, Washington added a fourteenth of his own: "Sufficient Powers to Congress for general purposes!" The custom of the thirteen toasts has been all but forgotten, but was recently revived at the Genesee Country Museum in Mumford, New York, as part of the local Fourth of July observation.

Toasting not only transferred easily to North America but was enhanced by the skill of various practitioners including some of America's early leaders. If not the best, Benjamin Franklin certainly ranked with them. A number of his toasts have been recalled but none more often than one he delivered at Versailles while American emissary to France. On this occasion the toasting was led off by the British ambassador, who said, "George the Third, who, like the sun in its meridian, spreads a luster throughout and enlightens the world." The next toast came from the French minister, who said, "The illustrious Louis the Sixteenth, who, like the moon, sheds his mild and benevolent rays on and influences the globe." Franklin finished the round: "George Washington, commander of the American armies, who, like Joshua of old, commanded the sun and the moon to stand still, and both obeyed."

Other influences were at work in the transfer of America. Around 1800 there was a high-spirited drinking club in London known as the Anacreontic Society, which met at the Crown and Anchor tavern. It was named for the Greek poet Anacreon, who was known for poems that praised love and wine. Each meeting opened with a singing toast "To Anacreon in Heaven," which ended with these joyous lines:

> While thus we agree,
> Our toast let it be.
> May our club flourish happy, united and free!
> And long may the sons of Anacreon entwine,
> The myrtle of Venus with Bacchus's vine!

The composition became popular enough that a number of Americans learned it. On several occasions the tune was used to accommodate lyrics written in America. One of these writers was Francis Scott Key, who found it the perfect vehicle for his "Star-Spangled Banner."

If there was a Golden Age for toasting it came during the period from approximately 1880 to 1920. Scores of toast books and pamphlets came on the market; prominent authors wrote and contributed their own for anthologies, newspapers ran columns of them, and one periodical, *The National Magazine,* actually had its own Toast Editor, whose duties included judging the winners of its monthly toasting contest. Several writers of the period, such as Fred Emerson Brooks and Minna

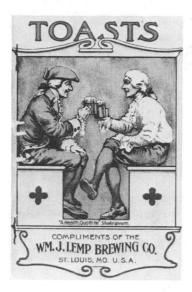

Brewer's Toasts.
The cover of booklet of
toasts given out by
a St. Louis brewery.
*(Warshaw Collection,
the Smithsonian)*

Thomas Antrim, built considerable reputations as toast
writers and the great comic poets of the time, like Oliver Herford and Wallace Irwin, created dozens of mar-
velous invitations to drink. One of Herford's many
champagne toasts, "The bubble winked at me and said,
'You'll miss me, brother, when you're dead.' "

Toasts were written for every imaginable institution
and situation—cities, colleges, states, holidays, baseball
teams, fools, failures, short people, and fat people. A
British collection contained a toast, several pages in
length, written for "The Opening of an Electric Gener-
ating Station." Occupational toasts were very popular,
and some clubs and fraternal organizations opened
their dinners with a toast to each of the professions
represented at the table. Many of these incorporated
one or more atrocious pun. Thus almost everyone was
given their due:

> **The Grocer**—Whosehonestteaisthebestpolicy!
> **The Paper Hanger**—Who is always up against
> it and still remains stuck up!
> **The Conductor**—May he always know what is
> fare!

The Author—The queerest of animals; their tales come out of their head!

The Baker—Who loafs around all day and still makes the dough! (or, May he never be done so much as to make him crusty!)

The Glazier—Who takes panes to see his way through life!

The Actor—A paradox who plays when he works and works when he plays!

Undertakers—May they never overtake us!

Blacksmiths—Success to forgery!

This was also a time for longer, more elaborate toasts. Some were long, florid, and overblown, which no doubt put as many to sleep as were entertained. Some of these toast-essays, however, had some punch, such as this one that took first prize in one of the *National Magazine*'s contests for 1911. The toast, entitled "The Way of a Woman," was submitted by Miss Saidee Lewis:

She was sweet and soft and clinging, and he always found her singing when he came home from his labors as the night was closing in; she was languishing and slender, and he simply couldn't tell her that her coffee was a sin. Golden hair her head was crowning; she was fond of quoting Browning, and she knew a hundred legends of the olden, golden time; and her heart was full of yearning for the Rosicrucian learning, and he simply couldn't tell her that the beefsteak was a crime. She was posted on Pendennis, and she knew the songs of Venice, and he listened to her prattle with an effort to look pleased; and she liked the wit of Weller—and he simply couldn't tell her that the eggs he had for breakfast had been laid by hens diseased. So she filled his home with beauty, and she did her wifely duty; did it as she understood it, and her conscience didn't hurt, when dyspepsia boldly sought him, and the sexton came and got him, and his tortured frame was buried 'neath a wagonload of dirt.

Oh those marriagable misses, thinking life all

love and kisses, mist and moonshine, glint and glamour, stardust borrowed from the skies! Man's a gross and sordid lummox—men are largely made of stomachs, and the songs of all the sirens will not take the place of pies!

There were also political and military toasts of near epic proportions. An anti-Teddy Roosevelt toast, "No! Teddy Don't Play Fair," drones on for eleven stanzas before it gets to the point:

> But honest old Bill Bryan,
> With kindliness will wear
> Away all Republican lyin'
> No! Teddy don't play fair.

Ironically, a number of toasts were written in honor of the teetotaling Bryan, who nonetheless managed in social situations. Bryan once found himself in a position where he was called on to toast the British navy. He lifted his glass of water and said, "Gentlemen, I believe all your victories were won on water."

A toast which was written in honor of Alton B. Parker after his unsuccessful bid for the presidency in 1904 is also typical of the period—if nothing else, it rhymes:

> It's a pardonable pride a Democrat feels
> For Alton B. Parker, Court of Appeals,
> He bore our standard last campaign,
> And although his fight was in vain,
> Alton B. Parker, you're alright.
> Alton B. Parker, may your skies be bright.

When Prohibition went into effect in 1920, the drinking continued, but the customs changed. A writer who was trying to reintroduce toasting and other traditional drinking customs in 1934 after repeal put it this way: "When Prohibition placed its stranglehold on our nation, it doomed for more than thirteen years the real art and etiquette of drinking."

Not only were wine, beer, and spirits on the banned

Men's Bar. This image is from an old magic lantern slide presentation on temperance. As the show progresses, the gent being toasted in this picture slides into habitual drunkenness but is saved at the end by Prohibitionists. *(Author's collection)*

list, but so for all practical purposes the formularies, books, ads, and magazine articles that helped carry the lore and customs of drinking. A good bootlegger could get a few bottles of champagne (or a reasonable facsimile) for a wedding, but no publishers were bootlegging collections of wedding toasts. Banquets, large open parties, and many of the other functions where one used to go to have a drink or two and launch a few toasts were now scarce and usually dry. Places where one would go for a leisurely drink to toast the health of a friend's new baby—the corner saloon, the cocktail lounge, and the hotel bar—were shut down for the duration and replaced by dank speakeasies where one would slink to have a fast drink of questionable origin.

All of this is not to say that people did not toast, but in many cases their toasts' substance had to do with the Volstead Act, the antisaloonists, and the quality of bathtub gin. For example:

> Here's to prohibition,
> The devil take it!
> They've stolen our wine,
> So now we make it.*

At the very moment of repeal there was a lot of toasting, which for the most part was addressed to the act itself; but after this initial flurry, the custom of the toast continued the decline begun during Prohibition. There were, of course, many who continued the tradition, and from time to time new toasts appeared as did these two examples respectively from the 1930s and 1950s:

> Here's to the new radio—
> Here's to our neighbor's loudspeaker
> So loud we need none of our own
> May its volume never grow weaker.

> Here's to today!
> For tomorrow we may be radioactive.

Fortunately, there have been a few who have gone against the trend, so all is not lost. Like those who carried the seeds of the Renaissance through the time of Darkness, and like others who have gone against the cultural tide, we have:

· **The McElvy Legacy.** When New Yorker Douglas McElvy passed away in 1973, he left $12,000 for his friends to toast him on the anniversary of his death. The cash lasted for three years, but his friends still meet each New Year's Day at the bar where the legacy was drained to pour him a memorial gin and tonic and toast his empty stool.

· **The Cogswellians.** A society of self-styled bon vivants who assemble each month in Washington, D.C., to honor the memory of an ardent Prohibitionist

---

*What aspires to be the definitive collection of Volstead era toasts appears in the main section of this book under the heading *Prohibition.*

named Cogswell who left water-dispensing monuments to the abstemious spirit. The Cogswellian's toast: "Temperance. I'll drink to that!"

· **The McGowan Influence.** If there is one place in the world today where the custom is doing well, it is Ireland. Jack McGowan, an affable man who is with the Irish Distillers International in Dublin, has collected toasts and Irish blessings over the years. He has made it his policy to share this treasury with interested parties in so-called civilized areas of the world where the custom is presently out of style. Toasts from McGowan's collection have shown up in American newspaper columns and form the bulk of the section of this book containing Irish toasts. Come the revival, McGowan's influence will be termed seminally important.

To get the Great Toast Revival off to a good start, the following pages contain some 1,200 of the best, most useful, and most literate toasts that could be found. With the help of dozens of people—reference librarians, museum curators, brewers, distillers, vintners, and old friends—I was able to collect something on the order of 5,000 different toasts from which the examples in this book were culled.

HOW TO USE
THIS BOOK

This book has been designed for both quick access and leisurely browsing. To accomplish both these ends, everything except for what has already appeared and the *Acknowledgments, Bibliography,* and *Index* have been alphabetized. So that anyone looking for *Hints for Effective Toasting,* a collection of *Historic Toasts,* as well as toasts having to do with *Health, Home,* or *Husbands* will be rewarded by looking under *H. L* yields *Love, Luck,* and *Lust* in that order—a good toast right there.

The *Contents, General Index, Author Index,* and generous use of *See also*'s conspire to help you find appropriate toasts quickly, which in turn should make you rich, famous, and popular beyond your wildest dreams.

Toasts and Toasting

Age

Do not resist growing old—Many are denied the privilege.

Fill high the goblet! Envious time steals, as we speak, our fleeting prime.

Here's a health to the future;
  A sigh for the past;
We can love and remember,
  And hope to the last,
And for all the base lies
  That the almanacs hold
While there's love in the heart,
  We can never grow old.

Here's that we may live to eat the hen,
That scratches on our grave.

Let him live to be a hundred! We want him on earth.

                    —Oliver Wendell Holmes
                    to a friend.

Long life to you and may you die in your own bed.

Old Friends. Genre photograph from the 1930s. *(Library of Congress)*

May our lives, like the leaves of the maple, grow
   More beautiful as they fade.
May we say our farewells, when it's time to go,
   All smiling and unafraid.
               —Larry E. Johnson.

May the Lord love us but not call us too soon.

May we keep a little of the fuel of youth to warm
   our body in old age.

May you enter heaven late.

May you live as long as you want, may you never want as long as you live.

May you live to be a hundred—and decide the rest for yourself.

The good die young—Here's hoping that you may live to a ripe old age.

To maturity:
When there's snow on the roof,
there's fire in the furnace.

To the Old Guard, the older we grow,
The more we take and the less we know.
At least the young men tell us so,
But the day will come, when they shall know
Exactly how far a glass can go,
To win the battle, 'gainst age, the foe.
Here's youth . . . in a glass of wine.
                    —James Monroe McLean,
                    The Book of Wine.

To the old, long life and treasure;
To the young, all health and pleasure.
                    —Ben Johnson.

You're not as young as you used to be
But you're not as old as you're going to be
So watch it!
                    —Irish.

SEE ALSO: *Birthday; Health; New Years.*

Alliterative

An alphabetical selection of this long-popular toast form. Many of these were regarded as old at the time of the American Revolution. Included at the end are two toast oddities in one: an orderly Jacobite offering and an acrostic.

Abundance, abstinence, and annihilation.
Abundance to the poor,
Abstinence to the intemperate,
Annihilation to the wicked.

Bachelors, banns, and buns.
Bachelors for the maidens,
Banns for the bachelors,
Buns after the consummation of the banns.*

Cheerfulness, content, and competency.
Cheerfulness in our cups,
Content in our minds,
Competency in our pockets.

The three good C's: conscience, claret and cash.

*Banns: the stated intention to marry.

Firmness, freedom and fortitude.
Firmness in the Senate,
Freedom on the land,
Fortitude on the waves.
Friendship, feeling and fidelity.
Friendship without interest,
Feeling to our enemies,
Fidelity to our friends.

The three H's: Health, Honor and Happiness.
Health to all the world,
Honor to those who seek for it,
Happiness in our homes.

The eight H's:
Handsome Husband,
Handsome House,
Health and Happiness,
Here and Hereafter.

Love, life and liberty.
Love pure,
Life long,
Liberty boundless.

Mirth, music and moderation.
Mirth at every board,
Music in all instruments,
Moderation in our desires.

Wine, wit and wisdom.
Wine enough to sharpen wit,
Wit enough to give zest to wine,
Wisdom enough to "shut down" at the right time.

The following, known as the Jacobite Toast, is ascribed to Lord Duff, who presented it in the year 1745.

A. B. C. . . .A Blessed Change.
D. E. F. . . .Down Every Foreigner.
G. H. J. . . .God Help James.
K. L. M. . . .Keep Lord Marr.

N. O. P. . . .Noble Ormond Preserve.
Q. R. S. . . .Quickly Resolve Stewart.
T. U. V. W. .Truss Up Vile Whigs.
X. Y. Z. . . .'Xert Your Zeal.

T riumphant eloquence that knows no depth,
O r height or width yet unattained—
A bject before your fiery strength we bow—
S pellbound—by glowing metaphor enchained.
T oward thee direct'd our strongest tribute is but
   weak
S ince tongues of men, not hearts, must speak.
                         —Henry Stanley Haskins.

America

Legend has it that sometime during the middle of the last century, three Americans were called on to toast their country at a dinner party in Paris. All were duly impressed with the size and growing importance of their country, and each tried to top the other in expressing his feelings. Here is the result:

1. Here's to the United States!—Bounded on the north by British America, on the south by the Gulf of Mexico, on the east by the Atlantic Ocean, and the west by the Pacific Ocean!

2. Here's to the United States!—Bounded on the north by the North Pole, on the south by the South Pole, on the east by the rising sun, and on the west by the setting sun.

3. I give you the United States!—Bounded on the north by the Aurora Borealis, on the south by the procession of the equinoxes, on the east by primeval chaos, and on the west by the Day of Judgment!

Other American toasts from various eras:

"The AMERICA"

A. WERNER & CO.
N.Y.

CHAMPAGNE.

ONANT & FULLER.

Patriotic Label. 19th-century champagne label. *(Warshaw Collection, the Smithsonian)*

A toast before we go:
Huzzah for America, ho!
Let us care for no man,
If no man cares for us.

America and England: and may they never have any
division but the Atlantic between them.
                                        —Charles Dickens.

America—half-brother of the world!—with something good and bad of every land.

—Philip Bayley.

Here's to the memory
Of the man
That raised the corn
That fed the goose
That bore the quill
That made the pen
That wrote the Declaration of Independence.

It is my loving sentiment, and by the blessing of God it shall be my dying sentiment—Independence now and Independence forever!

—Daniel Webster.

Let us ever remember that our interest is in concord, not in conflict; and that our real eminence rests in the victories of peace, not those of war.

—William McKinley,
at the Pan-American Exposition,
September 5, 1901.

May the enemies of America be destitute of beef and claret.

—18th century. The above toast and the two that follow come from an extremely early American toast book located in the rare-book collection of the Library of Congress. The book, *Everybody's Toast Book,* is undated but clearly from the late eighteenth or very early nineteenth century.

May the liberties of America never be clipped by the shears of bad economy.

May the world's wonder be American thunder.

One flag, one land, one heart, one hand, one nation evermore.

—Oliver Wendell Holmes.

Our country, Congress, cash, and courage.

Our country! When right, to be kept right. When wrong, to be put right!

—Carl Schurz, who was doubtlessly responding to a statement of Stephen Decatur that was a very popular toast for many years and which became a rallying cry for supporters of U.S. government policies during the Vietnam War.

Decatur's toast:
Our country! In her intercourse with foreign nations, may she always be in the right; but our country right or wrong.

To our country! Lift your glasses!
To its sun-capped mountain passes,
To its forests, to its streams,
To its memories, its dreams,

To its laughter, to its tears,
To the hope that after-years
Find us plodding on the way
Without so much tax to pay.

To Uncle Sam:
Addition to his friends,
Subtraction from his wants,
Multiplication of his blessings,
Division among his foes.

SEE ALSO: *Historic; Military.*

Anniversaries

Here is to loving, to romance, to us.
May we travel together through time.
We alone count as none, but together we're one,
For our partnership puts love to rhyme.

— Irish.

Here's to you both—
a beautiful pair,
on the birthday
of your love affair.

Let anniversaries come and let anniversaries go—but
may your happiness continue on forever.

May the warmth of our affections survive the frosts of
age.

To your coming anniversaries—may they be outnum-
bered only by your coming pleasures.

We've holidays and holy days, and memory days ga-
lore; And when we've toasted every one, I offer just one
more. So let us lift our glasses high, and drink a silent

Wedding Toast. Depression era photograph by John Vachon. *(Library of Congress)*

toast—The day, deep buried in each heart, that each one loves the most.

SEE ALSO: *Wedding.*

Babies/Children

A baby will make love stronger, days shorter, nights longer, bankroll smaller, home happier, clothes shabbier, the past forgotten, and the future worth living for.

A new life begun,
Like father, like son.
or
Like one, like the other,
Like daughter, like mother.

A generation of children on the children of your children.

—Irish.

A lovely being scarcely formed or molded,
A rose with all its sweetest leaves yet folded.
—Lord Byron.

Every baby born into the world is a finer one than the last.

—Charles Dickens,
Nicholas Nickleby.

Grandchildren are gifts of God.
  It is God's way . . .
Of compensating us for growing old.
                              —Irish.

Here's to the baby—man to be—
  May he be as fine as thee!
Here's to baby—woman to be—
  May she be as sweet as thee!

Here's to the stork,
A most valuable bird,
That inhabits the residence districts.
He doesn't sing tunes,
Nor yield any plumes,
But he helps the vital statistics.

May he/she grow twice as tall as yourself and half
as wise.
                              —Irish.

So that our children will have wealthy parents.

"The stork has brought a little peach!"
  The nurse said with an air.
"I'm mighty glad," the father said,
  "He didn't bring a pear."

We haven't all the good fortune to be ladies; we have
not all been generals, or poets or statesmen; but when
the toast works down to the babies we stand on common ground. We've all been babies.
                              —Samuel L. Clemens.

SEE ALSO: *Parents.*

Vivite felices, succedant dulcia Curis pocula, quæque dies me sine tristis a bit.

"Bacchus and Two Children Embedded In Grapevines."
Line engraving, about 1680, signed S. Ju., published by Jean Le
Blond. *(The Christian Brothers Collection at the Wine Museum
of San Francisco)*

Beer/Ale

Ale's a strong wrestler,
Flings all it hath met;
And makes the ground slippery,
Though it not be wet.

Beer! Beer! Beer!
We students do adore you,
Beer! Beer! Beer!
We love to see you foam;
When we for wine abjure you,
We miss you we assure you,
For it's only with clear sparkling beer
That students feel at home.

Come, sit we by the fireside
And roundly drink we here,
Till that we see our cheeks all dyed
And noses tanned with beer.
          —Robert Herrick.

Here's to the best ale in the best ale.
        —Mr. Pickwick,
           from Charles Dickens's
           The Pickwick Papers.

Lemp's Toasts. Booklet of toasts including those promoting the brewery that compiled them. *(Warshaw Collection, the Smithsonian)*

Here,
With my beer
I sit,
While golden moments flit;
Alas!
They pass
Unheeded by;

Beer Drinker. Old advertising card. *(Warshaw Collection, the Smithsonian)*

And as they fly,
I,
Being dry,
Sit, idly sipping here
My beer.
        —George Arnold.

Let's drink the liquid of amber so bright;
Let's drink the liquid with foam snowy white;
Let's drink the liquid that brings all good cheer;
Oh, where is the drink like old-fashioned beer?
                —A popular 19th-century
                toast often adapted to
                the use of a particular
                brand such as the follow-
                ing from a St. Louis
                brewery:

Let's drink the liquid of amber so bright;
Let's drink the liquid with foam snowy white;
Let's drink the liquid that brings all good cheer;
Oh, where is the drink like Lemp's Lager Beer?

None so deaf as those who will not hear.
None so blind as those who will not see.
But I'll wager none so deaf nor blind that he
Sees not nor hears me say come drink this beer.
                —W. L. Hassoldt.

Who'd care to be a bee and sip
Sweet honey from the flower's lip
When he might be a fly and steer
Head first into a can of beer?

SEE ALSO: *Libations; Revelry; Spirits.*

— 53 —

Better Times

A speedy calm to the storms of life.

Bury the blue devils.*

Here's a health to poverty; it sticks by us when our friends forsake us.

Here's to thee, my honest friend,
Wishing these hard times to mend.

If the world is going wrong,
    Forget it!
Sorrow never lingers long—
    Forget it!
If your neighbor bears ill-will,
If your conscience won't be still,
If you owe an ancient bill,
    Forget it!

---

*The old, original version is longer:

Come fill the bowl, each jolly soul;
    Let Bacchus guide our revels;
Join cup to lip, with "hip, hip, hip,"
    And bury the blue devils.

"La Vivandière." Katie the wineseller brings drink to bedraggled soldiers. Lithograph by Jean Henri Marlet (1770–1847). *(The Christian Brothers Collection at the Wine Museum of San Francisco)*

Laugh and the world laughs with you;
Weep, and it gives you the laugh anyway.

Let us make our glasses kiss;
Let us quench the sorrow-cinders.
> —Ralph Waldo Emerson,
> in *The Persian of Hafiz,*
> 1851.

May poverty always be a day's march behind us.

May the sunshine of comfort dispel the clouds of despair.

May we ever be able to part with our troubles to advantage.

Remember the poor—it costs nothing.
                                        —Josh Billings.

To the Great Unknown—who is waiting to do us a favor.

SEE ALSO: *General; Luck; Past, Present, and Future.*

Biblical

The Bible does not give us any direct mention of toasting, but there are a number of passages that indicate that the custom was observed. Even an antitoast cleric of the last century had to concede: "It is hardly probable that Ben-hadad and the thirty-two kings, his companions, would drink themselves drunk in the pavilions without some interchange of courtesies" (see I Kings 20:16).

A number of lines from the Bible have been used as toasts, including these:

A feast is made for laughter, and wine maketh merry.
—Ecclesiastes 10:19.

Drink no longer water, but use a little wine for thy stomach's sake.
—I Timothy 5:23.

Eat thy bread with joy, and drink thy wine with a merry heart.
—Ecclesiastes 9:7.

Forsake not an old friend, for the new is not comparable to him. A new friend is as new wine: when it is old, thou shalt drink it with pleasure.

—Ecclesiastes 9:10.

Give . . . wine unto those that be of heavy hearts.
—Proverbs 31:6.

The best wine . . . that goeth down sweetly, causing the lips of those that are asleep to speak.

—Song of Solomon 7:9.

Wine maketh glad the heart of man.
—Psalms 104:15.

Wine nourishes, refreshes and cheers. Wine is the foremost of all medicines . . . wherever wine is lacking, medicines become necessary.

—The Talmud.

Toast from Genesis. Many, many centuries after the fact, an artist drew this scene to represent the feast of Abraham at the birth of his child.

Wine was created from the beginning to make men joyful, and not to make men drunk. Wine drunk with moderation is the joy of the soul and the heart.

—Ecclesiasticus 31:35–36.

Wine, which cheereth God and man.

—Judges 9:13.

SEE ALSO: *Food.*

Birthdays

A health, and many of them. Birthdays were never like this when I had 'em.

Although another year is past
He's/She's no older than the last!

Another candle on your cake?
Well, that's no cause to pout.
Be glad that you have strength enough
To blow the damn thing out.

Another year older? Think this way:
Just one day older than yesterday!

God grant you many and happy years,
  Till, when the last has crowned you,
The dawn of endless days appears,
  And heaven is shining round you!
                —Oliver Wendell Holmes.

Happy birthday to you
  And many to be,
With friends that are true
  As you are to me!

Here's to you! No matter how old you are, you don't
look it!

Many happy returns of the day of your birth:
Many blessings to brighten your pathway on earth;
Many friendships to cheer and provoke you to
    mirth:
Many feastings and frolics to add to your girth.
                                    —Robert H. Lord.

May you live to be a hundred years with one extra year
to repent.
                                    —Irish.

Time marches on!
Now tell the truth—
Where did you find
The fountain of youth?

To wish you joy on your birthday
And all the whole year through,
For all the best that life can hold
Is none too good for you.

To your birthday, glass held high,
Glad it's you that's older—not I.

SEE ALSO: *Age; Health.*

Bulls

This term for absurd contradictions—e.g., "It's a mighty good thing for your wife that you're not married"—goes back at least to the thirteenth century and Chaucer's *bole*. Some that have become toasts:

A toast to posterity—though it does nothing for us.

Here's to abstinence—as long as it's practiced in moderation.

Here's to _____, equal to none.

Here's to the glorious _____, the last in the fight and the first out.

Here's to your wedding and many of them.

I hope you are all here to do honor to the toast. As many of ye as is present will say, "Here!" and as many of ye as is not present will say, "Absent!"

Liberty all over the world, and everywhere else.

May every patriot love his native country, whether he was born in it or not.

To our health. May it remain with us long after we die.

Celia's Toast
(with variations)

Drink to me only with thine eyes,
  And I will pledge with mine;
Or leave a kiss but in the cup,
  And I'll not look for wine.
          —Ben Johnson,
          "To Celia."

Drink to me only with thine eyes,
  And I will pledge with mine;
For I would have to pledge my watch
  If she should drink more wine.

Drink to me only with thine eyes,
  And I will pledge with mine;
Or, leave a kiss within the cup—
  I'll wash it down with wine.

Drink to me only with thine eyes?
I'll take a little wine.
  The eyes we prize
  Are full of lies,
I'll none of that in mine.

Champagne

Here's champagne to your real friends and real pain to our sham friends.

Here's to champagne, the drink divine,
That makes us forget all our troubles;
It's made of a dollar's worth of wine
And three dollars' worth of bubbles.*

If ever . . . in the eternal times that are to come, you and I shall sit down in Paradise, in some little shady corner by ourselves; and if we shall by any means be able to smuggle a basket of champagne there (I won't believe in a Temperance Heaven), and if we shall then cross our celestial legs in the celestial grass that is forever tropical, and strike our glasses and our heads together, till both musically ring in concert,—then, O my dear fellow-mortal, how shall we pleasantly discourse of all the things manifold which now so distress us,—when all the earth shall be but a reminiscence, yea, its final dissolution an antiquity.
> —Herman Melville to Nathaniel Hawthorne.

---

*This is the original version of this toast, at least eighty years old, so you may want to inflate the dollar amounts to update it.

Champagne Toast. Advertising card, c. 1900. *(Warshaw Collection, the Smithsonian)*

O thrice accursed
Be a champagne thirst,
When the price of beer's all we've got.

Some take their gold
In minted mold,
And some in harps hereafter,
But give me mine
In bubbles fine
And keep the change in laughter.
—Oliver Herford.

The bubble winked at me and said,
"You'll miss me, brother, when you're dead."
—Oliver Herford.

SEE ALSO: *Wine; Libations; Revelry.*

Cheeses

CAMEMBERT

Soft, aromatic, ammoniacal,
Angelic half, half demoniacal;
We pledge thee, Camembert,
   The Rare:
Thou apotheosis of decay.
                    —W.E.P. French.

GENERAL

Cheese—milk's leap toward immortality.
                    —Clifton Fadiman.

LIMBERGER

The rankest compound of villainous smell
That ever offended nostril.
                    —Shakespeare.

ROQUEFORT

O Roquefort! We accept thee,
With no dissenting note,
As nature's sole apology
For having made the goat.
                    —W.E.P. French.

Christmas

A Christmas wish—
May you never forget
what is worth remembering
or remember
what is best forgotten.
                    —Irish.

Apple pie and Simon Beer,
Christmas comes but once a year.
                    —Old Southern saying.

At Christmas play and make good cheer
For Christmas comes but once a year.
                    —Thomas Turner.

Be merry all, be merry all,
With holly dress the festive hall,
Prepare the song, the feast, the ball,
To welcome Merry Christmas.

Here's to the holly with its bright red berry.
Here's to Christmas, let's make it merry.

Here's to the day of good will, cold weather, and
    warm hearts!

Here's to us all!
God bless us every one!
            —Tiny Tim's toast,
                from Charles Dickens's
                A Christmas Carol.

Or, for those would like to savor the entire incident:

At last the dinner was all done, the cloth was cleared,
the hearth swept, and the fire made up. The compound
in the jug being tasted, and considered perfect, apples
and oranges were put upon the table, and a shovelful
of chestnuts on the fire. Then all the Cratchit family
drew around the hearth in what Bob Cratchit called a
circle, meaning half a one; and at Bob Cratchit's elbow
stood the family display of glass. Two tumblers and a
custard-cup without a handle. These held the hot stuff
from the jug, however, as well as golden goblets would
have done; and Bob served it out with beaming looks,
while the chestnuts on the fire sputtered and cracked
noisily. Then Bob proposed:
    "A Merry Christmas to us all, my dears. God bless
us!"
    Which the family re-echoed.
    "God bless us every one!" said Tiny Tim, the last of
all.
            —Charles Dickens,
                A Christmas Carol.

Here's wishing you more happiness
Than all my words can tell,
Not just alone for Christmas
But for all the year as well.

Holly and ivy hanging up
And something wet in every cup.
                    —Irish.

I have always thought of Christmas as a good time; a

kind, forgiving, generous, pleasant time; a time when men and women seem by one consent to open their hearts freely; and so I say "God bless Christmas."
—Charles Dickens.

I know I've wished you this before
But every year I wish it more.
A Merry Christmas.
—From an old postcard.

I wish you a Merry Christmas
And a Happy New Year
A pocket full of money
And a cellar full of beer!

Joy to the world—and especially to you.

May the Virgin and her Child lift your latch on Christmas night.

—Irish. This refers to the old Irish custom of leaving the door unbolted and a candle in the window for Mary on her way to Bethlehem.

May you be as contented as Christmas finds you all the year round.
—Irish.

May you be poor in misfortune this Christmas
and rich in blessings
slow to make enemies
quick to make friends
and rich or poor, slow or quick,
as happy as the New Year is long.
—Irish.

May you be the first house in the parish to welcome St. Nicholas.
—Irish.

May you never be without a drop at Christmas.
—Irish

May your corn stand high as yourself, your fields grow
bigger with rain, and the mare know its own way home
on Christmas night.
—Irish.

May your sheep all have lambs
but not on Christmas night.
—Irish.

Now thrice welcome Christmas
Which brings us good cheer,
Minced pies and plum porridge.

Peace and plenty for many a Christmas to come.
—Irish.

The season when fowl murder promotes peace and
good will.

Then let us be merry and taste the good cheer,
And remember old Christmas but comes once a year.
—From an old Christmas carol.

'Twas the month after Christmas,
And Santa had flit;
Came there tidings for father
Which read: "Please remit!"

Cities and Towns

Time was when almost every city had at least one toast
in its honor. A sampling:

BOSTON

And this is good old Boston,
The home of the bean and the cod,
Where the Lowells talk to the Cabots,
And the Cabots talk only to God.
> —Dr. John C. Bossidy,
> at alumni dinner of
> Holy Cross College.

Then here's to the City of Boston
The town of the cries and the groans
Where the Cabots can't see the Kobotschniks
And the Lowells won't speak to the Cohns.
> —Franklin P. Adams,
> in *So Much Velvet.*

To self-satisfied Boston, always serene,
The land of the cultured, the home of the bean,
Where the erudite policemen, patrolling their beats,
Have nothing to watch but the crooks in the streets.

CHICAGO

Chicago sounds rough to the maker of verse;
One comfort we have—Cincinnati sounds worse.
                              —Oliver Wendell Holmes.

Here's to Chicago, where everything dates from the
  Fair
Where they know the full value of good hot air
When there's prospect of business they'll always
  stand treat
For their hearts are as big as their women's feet.

Here's to dear old Chicago,
The home of the ham what 'am,
Where everyone speaks to his neighbor,
And nobody gives a damn.

HOLLYWOOD

Here's to Hollywood—
A place where people from Iowa
Mistake each other for movie stars.
                              —Fred Allen.

NEW HAVEN

Here's to the town of New Haven,
   The home of the truth and the light,
     Where God speaks to Jones,
     In the very same tones,
   That he uses with Hadley and Dwight.
                              —Dean Jones.

NEW HAVEN AND BOSTON

Here's to New Haven and Boston,
And the turf that the Puritans trod
In the rest of mankind little virtue they find
But they feel quite chummy with God.
                              —Walter Foster Angell.

NEW YORK

Vulgar of manner, overfed,
Overdressed and underbred;
Crazed with avarice, lust and rum,
New York, thy name's Delirium.
>—B. R. Newton,
>"Owed to New York," 1906.

"OUR TOWN"

Here's to our town—a place where people spend
money they haven't earned to buy things they
don't need to impress people they don't like.

Here's to the virgins of _____;
It's not very much we see of 'em.
Here's to those charming, beautiful girls;
Here's to them—all three of 'em.

PHILADELPHIA

All hail the tranquil village!
  May nothing jar its ease,
Where the spiders build their bridges
  From the trolleys to the trees.

To old Philadelphia, stately and slow;
As soon as you get there you're ready to go.
That peaceful city of the dead,
Where the greatest excitement is going to bed.

PITTSBURGH

Here's to Pittsburgh; and may it suit you
As it has sooted me!

SAN FRANCISCO

Here's to old 'Frisco, out on the Coast
The American Paris, her favorite boast
Once in every nine minutes
Just watch them and time it
They'll sing you that song of the glorious climate.

WASHINGTON, D.C.

First in war, first in peace, and last in the American
    League.

Colleges and Universities

GEORGIA TECH

I'd drink to ev'ry fellow who comes from far and
    near;
I'm a rambling wreck from Georgia Tech and a hell
    of an engineer!

HARVARD

   Here's to Johnny Harvard;
   Fill him up a full glass,
Fill him up a glass to his name and fame,
   And at the same time
   Don't forget his true love;
Fill her up a bumper to the brim.

M.I.T.

Of course I like the M.I.T.,
Jolly place for fun, you see,
You can work from nine to six by day,
And from seven to one, at night, they say,
And go to bed with an aching head
And a weary sense of work undone,

And a wonder strong as to where's the fun
If you study at M.I.T.

PRINCETON

I wish I had a barrel of rum
And sugar three hundred pounds,
With the chapel bell to put it in
And the clapper to stir it 'round,
I'd drink to the health of Nassau, boys,
And the girls both far and near,
For I'm a rambling rank of poverty,
And a son of a Gambolier.

VASSAR

And so you see, for old V.C.
Our love shall never fail.
Full well we know
That all we owe
to Matthew Vassar's ale!
> —Vassar song that refers to the
> Poughkeepsie ale brewer who
> founded the college.

YALE

For God, for Country and for Yale.

For we think it is but right, sir,
On Wednesday and Saturday night, sir.
To get most gloriously tight, sir,
    To drive dull care away.
It is a way we have at old Yale, sir,
    To drive dull care away.

Let him be kept from paper, pen and ink.
That he may cease to write and learn to think.

SEE ALSO: *Reunions; Special Occasions* (The Graduate).

"A Drinking Bout of Students." Line engraving by an anonymous German artist, c. 1800. *(The Christian Brothers Collection at the Wine Museum of San Francisco)*

Curses

A toast in reverse is a curse. In form, they are alike right down to the common openings of "Here's to . . ." and "May you . . ." Here, in English, is a sampling from the two great sources, Gaelic and Yiddish.

Here's to short shoes and long corns to our enemies.
—Irish.

May a band of gypsies camp in your belly and train
    bears to dance on your liver.
—Yiddish.

May his cradle ne'er rock, may his box have no
    lock,
May his wife have no frock for to cover her back,
May his cock never crow, may his bellows ne'er
    blow,
And his pipe and his pot, may he ever more lack.
—Irish,
    "To an informer."

May his pig never grunt, may his cat never hunt,
That a ghost may catch him in the dark of the
    night,

May his hen never lay, may his ass never bray,
And his goat fly away like an old paper kite.
>   —Irish.

May his spade never dig.
May his sow never pig.
May each hair in his wig be well thrashed with a
flail.
May his door never latch.
May his turkeys not hatch.
May the rats eat his mail.
May every old fairy from Cork to Dunleary dip him
snug and airy in river or lake where the eel and
the trout may dine on the snout of the monster
that murdered Nell Flaherty's Drake.
>   —One verse of Irish cursing song,
>   "Nell Flaherty's Drake."

May she marry a ghost, and bear him a kitten, and may
the high king of glory permit it to get the mange.
>   —Irish.

May the devil cut the toes off all our toes, that we may
know them by their limping.
>   —Irish.

May the devil make a ladder of your backbone while
he is picking apples in the garden of hell.
>   —Irish.

May you grow so rotten that goats, skunks, and pigs
refuse to be near you.
>   —Yiddish.

May you never develop stomach trouble from too rich
a diet.
>   —Yiddish.

May you turn into a sparrow and owe your existence
to the droppings of a horse.
>   —Yiddish.

That all your teeth should fall out—but one should remain for a toothache.

—Yiddish.

SEE ALSO: *Hell and Damnation.*

Death

Ah, make we the most of what we may yet spend,
Before we too into the Dust descend;
Dust into Dust, and under Dust to lie,
Sans wine, sans song, sans singer, and sans end
> —Omar Khayyam.

All care to the wind we merrily fling,
For the damp, cold grave is a dead sure thing!
It's a dead sure thing we're alive tonight
And the damp, cold grave is out of sight.
> —Ernest Jarrold
> (Toast of the Vampire Club)

Here's to death, because death will give me one last
bier.

Let the world slide, let the world go;
A fig for care, and a fig for woe;
If I can't pay, why I can owe,
And death makes equal the high and low.

May every hair on your head turn into a candle to
light your way to heaven, and may God and His

Holy Mother take the harm of the years away from you.

—Irish.

Oh, here's to other meetings,
　　And merry greetings then;
And here's to those we've drunk with,
　　But never can again.

Over their hallowed graves may the winds of heaven whisper hourly benedictions.

Though life is now pleasant and sweet to the sense
We'll be damnably mouldy a hundred years hence.

—Old pirate toast.

Time cuts down all,
Both great and small.

'Tis my will when I die, not a tear shall be shed,
No *Hic Jacet* be graved on my stone,
But pour o'er my coffin a bottle of red,
And write that *His Drinking is Done.*

To Death, the jolly old bouncer, now
　　Our glasses let's be clinking;
If he hadn't put other out, I trow,
　　To-night we'd not be drinking.

—Oliver Herford.

To live in hearts we leave behind, is not to die.

Wash me when dead in the juice of the vine, dear
　　friends!
Let your funeral service be drinking and wine, dear
　　friends!
And if you would meet me again when the
　　Doomsday comes,
Search the dust of the tavern, and sift from it mine,
　　dear friends!

(2) McCarthy's Wake. " May He Rest in Peace."

Wake. A not altogether flattering view of the grieving Irish as seen through the eyes of a Philadelphia photographer, c. 1900. *(Author's collection)*

England

Daddy Neptune, one day, to Freedom did say,
If ever I lived upon dry land,
The spot I would hit on would be little Britain!
Says Freedom, "Why that's my own island!"
O, it's a snug little island!
A right little, tight little island!
Search the world round, none can be found
So happy as this little island.

England! my country, great and free!
Heart of the world, I drink to thee!

In English beer,
With an English cheer,
To the right little,
Tight little island!

O England!—model to thy inward greatness,
Like little body with a mighty heart.
        —Shakespeare, *King Henry V,* Act II.

"Excuses for the Glass"

In Richard Brinsley Sheridan's comedy *The School for Scandal,* a character by the name of Sir Toby Bumper recites a toast that thereafter defined a particular kind of toast that is more the "excuse for the glass" than an expression of anything else.

Starting with the full version of Sheridan's toast, here is a collection of excuses dedicated to such concerns as fleas, riotous monks, and salt.

Here's to the maiden of bashful fifteen;
    Here's to the widow of fifty;
Here's to the flaunting extravagant quean,
    And here's to the housewife that's thrifty.
        Let the toast pass—
        Drink to the lass—
I'll warrant she'll prove an excuse for the glass.

Here's to the charmer whose dimples we prize;
    Now to the maid who has none, sir;
Here's to the girl with a pair of blue eyes,
    And here's to the nymph with but one, sir.
        Let the toast pass—
        Drink to the lass—

I'll warrant she'll prove an excuse for the glass.

Here's to the maid with a bosom of snow;
    Now to her that's as brown as a berry:
Here's to the wife with a face full of woe,
    And now for the damsel that's merry.
        Let the toast pass—
        Drink to the lass—
I'll warrant she'll prove an excuse for the glass.

For let 'em be clumsy, or let 'em be slim,
    Young or ancient, I care not a feather:
So fill a pint bumper quite up to the brim,
    And let us e'en toast 'em together.
        Let the toast pass—
        Drink to the lass—
I'll warrant she'll prove an excuse for the glass.
                        —Richard B. Sheridan,
                            The School for Scandal,
                        Act III, Scene III.

Confusion to the minions of vice.

Great fleas have lesser fleas,
    And these have less to bite 'em;
These fleas have lesser fleas,
    And so *ad infinitum.*
The great fleas themselves in turn,
    Have greater fleas to go on.
While these again have greater still,
    And greater still, and so on.

Here's to "just so much"—
It's what we love,
It's what we hate,
It's what we started with,
It's what we've got,
It's what we'll finish with,
It's what we want,
It's what we get,
It's what we never expect to get,
It's what we do,

The Conquering Power. Valentino toasts Alice Terry in the 1921 film. *(MOMA/Film Stills Archive)*

It's what we leave undone,
It's the amount of good in us,
It's all the bad in us,
It's what we hope for hereafter.
   —Jean C. Hayez.

Here's to the bee—the busy soul;
He has no time for birth control.
That's why it is, in times like these,
We have so many sons of bees!

Here's to the chigger,
The bug that's no bigger
Than the point of a pin;
But the bump that he raises
Itches like blazes,
And that's where the rub comes in.

Here's to the flea that jumped over me and bit the
   behind of my missus.

Here's to the happy, bounding flea:
You cannot tell the he from the she,
But he can tell, and so can she!
                    —Roland Young.

I used to know a clever toast,
   But pshaw! I cannot think it—
So fill your glass to anything
   And, bless your souls, I'll drink it.

May riotous monks have a double Lent.

May the skin of your bum never cover a drum.

May we never put our finger in another man's pie.

O Salt! good to put into almost anything to eat or drink.
What a piquancy you impart to a melon; how savory
is meat when touched by your magic; how you coerce
the best in milk and potatoes; how you awaken the
merry meditative oyster; how corn and cucumbers and
onions and fruits and tomatoes are sent to the palate
addressed with their true flavor. O Salt!

Shee's pretty to walke with:
And witty to talke with;
And pleasant too to think on.
But the best use of all
Is, her health is a stawle,
And helps us to make us drinke on.
                    —Sir John Suckling.

There's many a toast I'd like to say,
If I could only think it;
So fill your glass to anything,
And thank the Lord, I'll drink it!
                    —Wallace Irwin.

SEE ALSO: *Bulls; Limericks; Tongue-Twisters; World's Worst Toasts.*

Fishing

For some unexplained reason, relatively large numbers of fishing toasts exist while other sports and pastimes have inspired few of them.

A fisherman, 'twixt you and I
Will very seldom tell a lie—
Except when it is needed to
Describe the fish that left his view.

Behold the fisherman!
He riseth in the early morning
And disturbeth the whole household.

Enjoy thy stream, O harmless fish,
And when an angler for his dish,
    Through gluttony's vile sin,
Attempts, the wretch, to pull thee out,
God give thee strength, O gentle trout,
    To pull the rascal in.

Health to men,
And death to fish;
They're wagging their tails
That will pay for this.

Here's to Fishing—a grand delusion enthusiastically promoted by glorious liars in old clothes.

—Don Marquis.

Here's to the fish that I may catch;
So large that even I,
When talking of it afterward,
Will never need to lie.

Here's to our fisherman bold;
Here's to the fish he caught;
Here's to the one that got away,
And here's to the one he bought.

May the holes in your net be no bigger than your fish.

—Irish.

Rod and line: May they never part company.

The steady fisherman—who never "reels home."

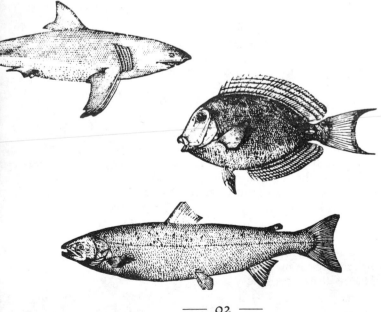

Food

A full belly, a heavy purse, and a light heart.

All human history attests
That happiness for man—the hungry sinner—
Since Eve ate apples, much depends on dinner!
                                        —Byron

Eat, drink and be merry for tomorrow you diet.

Good pies and strong beer.
                    —*Poor Robin's Almanack,* 1695.

Health to our bodies, peace to our minds, and plenty to
our boards.
                    —18th-century toast before dinner.

I'd rather have a dinner while I'm living than a monument when I'm dead, for the dinner will be on my
friends, while the monument would be on me.

"I was always religiously inclined,"
Said the oyster as he slid down
The minister's throat, "but ne'er
Did I dream I'd enter the clergy."

"The Hunt Breakfast." Etching dated 1787 by Thomas Rowlandson (1757–1827). *(The Christian Brothers Collection at the Wine Museum of San Francisco)*

Let the dogs wait a long time.
   —Irish wish for a lengthy
     and ample dinner.

May they have sugar to their strawberries!
       —Leigh Hunt,
          translated from an unidentified
          Italian poet, 1840.

O hour of all hours, the most blessed upon earth,
the blessed hour of our dinners!
               —Edward George Lytton.

On the table spread the cloth,
   Let the knives be sharp and clean;
Pickles get and salad both,
   Let them each be fresh and green.

With small beer, good ale, and wine,
O ye gods! how I shall dine!

Serenely full, the epicure would say,
Fate cannot harm me, I have dined today.

To eat, to drink, and to be merry.
                    —Ecclesiastes 8:15.

To Gasteria, the tenth Muse, who presides over the
enjoyments of Taste.
                    —Anthelme Brillat-Savarin.

To Mom's cooking:
May my wife never find out how bad it really was.

To soup: May it be seen and not heard.

Unquiet meals make ill digestions.
        — Shakespeare,
            The Comedy of Errors, Act V.

We may live without poetry, music and art,
We may live without conscience, and live without
    heart;
We may live without friends; we may live without
    books;
But civilized man cannot live without cooks.
We may live without books—what is knowledge but
    grieving?
We may live without hope—what is hope but
    deceiving?
We may live without love—what is passion but
    pining?
But where is the man that can live without dining?
                    —Owen Meredith, from "Lucile."

SEE ALSO: *Cheeses; Graces; Professional and Occupational* (Cooking).

Friendship

A day for toil, an hour for sport,
But for a friend life is too short.
　　　　　—Ralph Waldo Emerson.

A health to you,
A wealth to you,
And the best that life can give to you.
May fortune still be kind to you.
And happiness be true to you,
And life be long and good to you,
Is the toast of all your friends to you.

Absent friends—though out of sight we recognize them
with our glasses.

Don't walk in front of me,
　I may not follow.
Don't walk behind me,
　I may not lead.
Walk beside me,
　And just be my friend.
　　　　　—Irish.

Friendship's the wine of life.
Let's drink of it and to it.

Here's all that's fine to you!
Books and old wine to you!
Girls be divine to you!
       —Richard Hovey.

Here's to a friend. He knows you well and likes you just
the same.

Here's to beefsteak when you're hungry,
Whiskey when you are dry,
Greenbacks when you are busted,
And Heaven when you die!

Old Acquaintance. From the 1943 film with Bette Davis and
Miriam Hopkins. *(MOMA/Film Stills Archive)*

Here's to cold nights, warm friends, and a good drink to give them.

Here's to Eternity—may we spend it in as good company as this night finds us.

Here's to our friendship;
May it be reckoned
Long as a lifetime,
Close as a second.

Here's to the four hinges of Friendship—
Swearing, Lying, Stealing, and Drinking.
When you swear, swear by your country;
When you lie, lie for a pretty woman;
When you steal, steal away from bad company;
And when you drink, drink with me.

Here's to you, old friend, may you live a thousand
    years,
Just to sort of cheer things in this vale of human
    tears;
And may I live a thousand too—a thousand—less a
    day,
'Cause I wouldn't care to be on earth and hear you'd
    passed away.

May the friends of our youth be the companions of our old age.

May the hinges of friendship never rust,
nor the wings of love lose a feather.
                —Dean Ramsay,
                    in *Reminiscences of Scottish Life.*

May we have more and more friends,
and need them less and less!

May we never have friends who, like shadows, follow us in sunshine only to desert us on a cloudy day.

May your tobacco never run out, your library never
turn musty, your cellar never go dry, and your friends
never turn foes.

Now I, friend, drink to you, friend,
    As my friend drank to me,
And I, friend, charge you, friend,
    As my friend charged me,
That you, friend, drink to your friend,
    As my friend drank to me;
And the more we drink together, friend,
    The merrier we'll be!

Old friends are scarce,
New friends are few;
Here's hoping I've found
One of each in you.

Pour deep the rosy wine and drink a toast with me:
Here's to the three: Thee, Wine, and Camaraderie!
                                    —Tom Moore.

The world is gay and colorful,
And life itself is new.
And I am very grateful for
The Friend I found in you.

Then here's to thee, old friend; and long
    May thou and I this meet,
To brighten still with wine and song
    This short life ere it fleet.

To friends: as long as we are able
To lift our glasses from the table.

To my friend. If we ever disagree, may you be in
the right.

To our best friends, who know the worst about us but
refuse to believe it.

We'll think of all the friends we know
And drink to all worth drinking to.

We'll drink the wanting into wealth,
And those that languish into health,
The afflicted into joy, the oppressed
Into serenity and rest.
                              —Charles Cotton.

Were't the last drop in the well,
    As I gasp'd upon the brink,
Ere my fainting spirit fell,
    'Tis to thee I would drink.

SEE ALSO: *Alliterative; Biblical; General; Guests; Hosts/Hostesses;
Love; Old Things; Parting.*

General

Toasts of good will and good times.

A handsome new nose to you.

A little health, a little wealth,
    A little house and freedom:
With some few friends for certain ends
    But little cause to need 'em.

A toast to the wise
    And a toast to the foolish
A toast to your eyes—
    May they never grow mulish!

All that gives you pleasure.

All true hearts and sound bottoms.

And fill them high with generous juice,
As generous as your mind,
And pledge me in the generous toast—
The whole of human kind!
                              —Robert Burns.

Blue skies and green lights.

Days of Ease and Nights of Pleasure.

Delicious nights to every virtuous heart.

Good company, good wine, good welcome, make good
people.

—Shakespeare.

Good day, good health, good cheer, good night!

Health to my body, wealth to my purse
Heaven to my soul, and I wish you no worse.

Heaven give thee many, many merry days.
—Shakespeare.

Here's a toast to all who are here,
No matter where you're from;
May the best day you have seen
Be worse than your worst to come.

Here's hoping how and hoping who
And hoping when and where;
And may all good things come to you
Before you cease to care.

Here's to a long life, and a merry one,
A quick death, and a painless one,
A pretty woman, and a loving one,
A cold bottle, and another one!

Here's to all of us.
—Sir Thomas Lipton.

Here's to beauty, wit, and wine, and to a full stomach, a full purse, and a light heart.

Here's to the 'ealth o' your Royal 'ighness; hand my the skin o' ha gooseberry be big enough for han humbrella to cover up hall your enemies.
—Caddy's toast in "Erminie."

Here's to us that are here, to you that are there, and the rest of us everywhere.
—Rudyard Kipling.

Here's to your good health,
and your family's good health,
and may you all live long and prosper.
—Joseph Jefferson, actor,
as Rip Van Winkle.

Here's tow'ds yer an' tew yer!
'F I never had met yer
I'd never hev knewed yer.

I drink to the days that are.
—William Morris.

I wish thee health,
I wish thee wealth,
I wish thee gold in store,
I wish thee heaven upon earth—
What could I wish thee more?

Life is a jest, and all things show it—
I thought so once, but now I know it.
—John Gay.

Love to one, friendship to many, and good will to all.

Make the most of life while you may,
Life is short and wears away!
—William Oldys.

To Love's Limit.

Here's to the love that I
        hold for thee;
May it day by day grow stronger:
May it last as long as
        your love for me —
And not one second
        longer!

N. Fontaine B

"To Love's Limit." A prime example of the ornate page layout found in turn-of-the-century toast books. From a book entitled *Toasts for the Times in Pictures and Rhymes. (Author's collection)*

May our faults be written on the seashore, and every good action prove a wave to wash them out.

May our feast days be many and our fast days be few.
                                                —Mary L. Booth.

May the clouds in your life form only a background for a lovely sunset.

May the most you wish for be the least you get.

May we all live in pleasure and die out of debt.

May we be happy and our enemies know it.

May we live respected and die regretted.

May we breakfast with Health, dine with Friendship, crack a bottle with Mirth, and sup with the goddess Contentment.

May we live to learn well,
And learn to live well.

May we never do worse.

May we never feel want, nor ever want feeling.

May we never flatter our superiors or insult our inferiors.

May you always distinguish between the weeds and the flowers.

May you be merry and lack nothing.
—Shakespeare.

May you have the hindsight to know where you've been . . . The foresight to know where you're going . . . and the insight to know you've gone too far.
—Charles M. Meyers.

May you live all the days of your life.
—Jonathan Swift.

May you live as long as you want to and want to as long as you live.

Success to the lover, honor to the brave,
Health to the sick, and freedom to the slave.

The riotous enjoyment of a quiet conscience.

The three generals in power: General Employment,
General Industry, and General Comfort.

There is no satiety
In our society
With the variety
Of your *esprit.*
Here's a long purse to you,
And a great thirst to you!
Fate be no worse to you
Than she's been to me!

'Tis hard to tell which is best,
Music, Food, Drink, or Rest.

'Tis not so bad a world,
As some would like to make it;
But whether good or whether bad,
Depends on how you take it.

To the old, long life and treasure;
To the young, all health and pleasure;
  To the fair, their face,
  With eternal grace;
And the rest, to be loved at leisure.
                    —Ben Johnson.

Two ins and one out—in health, wealth, and out of
debt.

While we live, let us live.

Wit without virulence, wine without excess, and wisdom without affection.

You shall and you shan't,
  You will and you won't,
You're condemned if you do,
  And you are damned if you don't.

Toast In Space. NASA astronaut Thomas P. Stafford (left) and Donald K. Slayton toast their Soviet counterparts during their visit to the Soyuz spacecraft during the historic Apollo-Soyuz rendezvous in space. Vodka labels have been affixed to tubes of Soviet soup for the historic international space toast, July, 1975. *(NASA photo)*

Special Section 1

Glossary of Toast and Tipple (selected)

Some special terms for special occasions.

all nations. A vile drink composed of the dregs of various casks to which strong beer was sometimes added. A glass of this stuff might contain the leavings at the bottoms of gin, rye, rum, and brandy casks.

beverage. Derives from the word *bever,* which is a drink taken between meals. There used to be bever days at Eton College, for instance, when extra beer was served to the students.

binder. The last drink of the evening. "One for the road."

bridal. We all know what this means, but what is interesting is that it comes from an old English custom of the "Bride-Ale" by which the bride was given the proceeds from the sale of ale at her wedding.

brimmer.   A glass so full that the liquid touches the brim. Although the liquid has climbed to the brim, there is a slight depression or hollow in the center of the surface. A *bumper* (see below) is a brimmer to which extra drops have been added to fill the hollow to a bump. The difference between a brimmer and a bumper can be demonstrated by floating a cork fragment on the surface. In a brimmer the cork will float to the edge, while it will sit in the middle of a bumper.

bumper.   A glass filled to the extreme. Bumpers are often used in toasting and sometimes taken in one draught. There are two explanations for the term:

1.   It comes from the French *au bon père,* or "good father," and is attributed to the medieval custom of dedicating the first cup of wine to the Pope.

2.   It comes from a glass filled so high that the liquid "bumps" up in the middle, higher in the center than at the brim. (See *brimmer.*)

comet wine.   Wine made during a year in which a major comet appeared. It was long supposed that such wine was superior and best suited for great occasions. This belief, usually wrong, probably took root in 1811 when a notable vintage and a great comet coincided.

drop. There are 60 drops in a teaspoon; 120 in a dessertspoon; 240 in a tablespoon; 480 in an ounce; 960 in a wineglass; 1,920 in a teacup; 3,840 in a breakfast-cup or tumbler; 7,680 in a pint; 15,360 in a quart; 61,440 in a gallon; 2,935,360 in a barrel; 3,870,720 in a hogshead. Its equivalent weight is .9493 grams. A drop is equal to a minim. (From *The Banquet Book* by Cuyler Reynolds, 1902.)

firkin. A nine-gallon cask.

flap-dragon. An Elizabethan drink with a flammable surface, ignited for hard drinkers to quaff in one fast gulp. Drinking these was called flap-dragoning, and there are several references to the custom in Shakespeare's works.

fob. Brewer's term for beer froth.

hob-nob. The quaint custom of sitting around the "hob," or projecting corner of a fireplace, and drinking.

loving cup. A massive common cup, passed from hand to hand as a token of peace. It usually has three handles. Today these are largely ornamental and used as trophies.

There are a number of stories purporting to state the origin of the loving cup. This one makes as much sense as the rest and is the most interesting explanation. It seems that King Henry V was out riding, became thirsty, and stopped at the door of a country inn for a cup of wine. The barmaid handed it to him by its single handle, forcing him to take it in both hands, thereby soiling his gloves. The king made up his mind that this would not happen again so he had a cup made with two handles, which he then had sent to the inn for his private use. When he next happened on the inn, he again ordered a cup of wine. The same barmaid served him, this time grasping the cup by its two handles. The problem was solved when he ordered a three-handled cup made.

minim. A drop. See *drop.*

Nebuchadnezzar. The largest size of champagne bottle, capable of holding 104 glasses. It is larger than the 83-glass *Balthazar*, 62-glass *Salmanazar*, 41-glass *Methusela*, 31-glass *Rehoboam*, 21-glass *Jeroboam* and 10-glass *Magnum.* Your standard *Bottle* holds a mere five glasses.

nip. One-sixth of a quartern (a 5-oz. measure).

noggin. An old ale measure for a quarter-pint. The word appears in old drinking songs such as one with this currently relevant line:

> Before we think of jogging,
> Let's take a cheerful noggin.

no heel taps. An old drinking injunction meaning to finish your glass—leave no dregs. A number of diverse explanations have been made for the term's origin of which the most logical appears in Atherton Fleming's *Gourmet's Book of Food and Drink:* "There can be little doubt that the term is derived from *to heel,* as supplied to a cask; that is, to tilt after the clear contents have been nearly drawn off, and at the time when the liquid starts to turn turbid. 'Heel taps' are therefore the residuum of liquid in an almost empty cask, and by analogy, the leavings in a glass when the best part of the liquor has been drunk."

pegging away. This term (as well as several others, such as "to bring down a peg," and "a peg lower") derives from the peg tankard that held two quarts of ale and was studded with eight equally-spaced pegs or pins so as to allow a half pint between each peg. The pegs were the innovation of King Edgar, who decreed them as a means of controlling drunkenness. Under Edgar's plan, a pegged cup hung by every vintner's and brewer's door. The customer was only supposed to drink to the next peg and give up a fine of a penny for every draught taken beyond the peg.

piggin. A drinking vessel made from a pig's skin. It is one of a number of leather vessels of yore including also the bombard, gaspin, and black jack. Other bygone vessels include the crinze (earthenware), the wooden mazer, and the quaich (silver or china). In former times, it seems that just about anything that you could find might end up as a cup. A writer of 1635 tells of all the predictable materials for drinking vessels, including old boots, and then adds, "We have, besides, cups made out of hornes of beasts, of cockernuts, of goords, of the eggs of ostriches; others made of the shells of diverse fishes, brought from the Indies and other places, and shining like mother-of-pearle."

pitcher. Pouring vessel originally made of leather and so called because it was lined with pitch to make it waterproof.

punch. Although used less specifically today, the word originally referred to a drink of five ingredients: liquor, water, lemon, sugar, and spice. It derives from the Hindu work *paunch,* which means five. The drink was brought to England at the end of the seventeenth century by naval officers coming back from East India.

puncheon. A wine measure equal to 2 tierces, or 84 gallons, or 336 quarts, or 672 pints.

roast. Different than a toast, *viz.,*

> When T stands for tender
> And R stands for rough
> You've the difference twixt a
> Toast and a Roast.
> —"Stanlicus."

sentiments. During the eighteenth and much of the nineteenth centuries, toasts addressed to women were known as sentiments.

stirrup cup. One for the road. The name given to the drink given to a departing guest whose feet were already in the stirrups.

teetotaler. Term comes from a pledge of a Michigan temperance society of the 1830s. Members were offered two pledges: one calling for moderate drinking, the other calling for total abstinence. Once on the membership rolls the moderates were identified as "O.P." for "Old Pledge," and "T-Total" if they swore off entirely. They were soon known as teetotalers.

toddy. A sweet drink of whiskey, water, and sugar that is often warmed. Toddy is a corruption of *taudi,* the Hindu name for a sweet palm juice.

tumbler. A common drinking glass that was originally a drinking horn unevenly weighted with lead at the bottom. This was done to encourage the drinker to drain the contents at one draught, as the vessel was so weighted that it could not be put down without tumbling over. The tumbler is believed to be of Saxon origin.

wet your whistle. To drink. The term reputedly came from an old Scottish custom of awarding a silver whistle to the winner of a drinking contest. These contests were decided when only one participant was left standing and able to blow the whistle. One such contest was won by a Scotch nobleman who bested a boastful Dane after several days and nights of drinking. Robert Burns wrote of the memorable contest:

> I sing of a Whistle, a Whistle of worth;
> I sing of a Whistle, the pride of the North
> Was brought to the Court of our good Scottish
>   King
> And long with this Whistle all Scotland shall
>   ring.

XXX. Part of an old system for indicating the strength of beer or liquor on a scale of X (mild) to XXXX (quite strong).

SEE ALSO: *Ultimate Toasts.*

Graces

Bless this food and us that eats it.
—Cowboy grace.

For a' Thou'st placed upon the table, we thank the
Lord, as weel's we're able.

For what we are about to receive, the Lord make us
truly thankful, for Christ's sake. Amen.
—Old English grace.

Good bread, good meat
Good God, let's eat!

Heavenly father bless us,
And keep us all alive;
There's ten of us for dinner
And not enough for five.

Give me a good digestion, Lord,
   And also something to digest;
Give me a healthy body, Lord,
   And sense to keep it at its best.
—Dr. Furse,
   Bishop of St. Albans.

May the good Lord take a liking to you—but not too soon!

May the holy Saints be about your bed, and about your board, from this time to the latter end—God help us all!

—Irish.

O thou that blest the loaves and fishes,
Look down upon these two poor dishes,
And tho' the murphies are but small,
O make them large enough for all,
For if they do our bellies fill
I'm sure it is a miracle.

Some have meat but cannot eat;
Some could eat but have no meat;
We have meat and can all eat;
Blest, therefore, be God for our meat.

—*The Selkirk Grace* found in the papers of Dr. Plume of Maldon, Essex, in a handwriting of about 1650. Another version, attributed to Robert Burns:

Some hae meat, and canna eat,
   And some wad eat that want it;
But we hae meat, and we can eat,
   And sae the Lord be thankit.

Thank the Lord for what we've getten,
If ther 'ad been mooar, mooar we shud hev etten.

Guest of Honor. Etching by William Henry Boucher after a painting by Walter Sadler. *(Library of Congress)*

Guests

Here's to our guest—
Don't let him rest.
But keep his elbow bending.
'Tis time to drink—
Full time to think
Tomorrow when you're mending.

May our house always be too small to hold all our
friends.

—Myrtle Reed.

Our house is ever at your service.

See, your guests approach:
Address yourself to entertain them sprightly,
And let's be red with mirth.
—Shakespeare,
The Winter's Tale, Act IV.

The ornament of a house is the guests who frequent it.

To Our Guest! A friend of our friend's is doubly our
friend. Here's to him.

SEE ALSO: *Friendship; General; Hosts/Hostesses; Parting.*

Health

Health! Eldest, most august of all
The blessed gods, on thee I call!
Oh, let me spend with thee the rest
Of mortal life, securely blest!

Here's a health to every one;
Peace on earth, and heaven won.

Here's to your health—a long life and an easy death to
you.

Here's to your 'health! You make age curious, Time
furious, and all of us envious.

That a doctor might never earn a dollar out of you
And that your heart may never give out.

—Irish.

"To Your Health." Late-19th-century toaster. *(Library of Congress)*

The health of the salmon to you:
a long life,
a full heart
and a wet mouth!

     —Irish.

SEE ALSO: *Alliterative; Friendship; General.*

Hell and Damnation

Here's to Hell!
May the stay there
Be as much fun as the way there!

Here's to Mephisto! Goodness knows
What we would do without him.
And, good Mephisto, do not spurn
Our toast with mocking laughter;
Nor yet the compliment return
But toasting us hereafter.
                —Oliver Herford.

Here's to the Pavement of Hell,
And the tiresome old teachers who talk it.
Observation has taught
That we shall not be caught
Entirely alone, when we walk it.

Here's to those who love us well—
Those who don't may go to Hell.
                —James Keene.

Here's to you
Here's to me

May we never disagree.
But, if we do,
to Hell with you—
and here's to me!

   Up friends, up!
   Tonight we sup,
Though tomorrow we die of revel!
   Rise for a toast,
   Though tomorrow we roast;
A Health to His Lordship, the Devil!

SEE ALSO: *Curses.*

Special Section 2

Hints for Effective Toasting

1. *Do it in a way that is most comfortable to you. You may remain seated.* Legend has it that it became acceptable to toast without standing in Britain during the reign of Charles II. The king allowed that this would be acceptable after he had risen in response to a toast in his honor while aboard the ship *Royal Charles* and bashed his head into a beam. A similar bashing to King William IV, when he was heir to the throne and toasted George IV while aboard a man-of-war, forever ended the custom of standing toasts in the Royal Navy.

2. *Don't mix toasts with other messages.* During World War II, at a banquet given by Marshal Joseph Stalin at the Russian embassy in Teheran, Stalin rose to his feet after Churchill, Roosevelt, and other leaders had been toasted. He grinned and made a quick, impromptu remark in Russian. Judging from the smiles on the faces

of the Russians present, it could only be concluded that he had come up with a witty and appropriate toast. As the Americans and British grabbed their glasses, the interpreter rose to say, "Marshal Stalin says the men's room is on the right."

3. *If you are in some position where you are likely to be called on, it is a good idea to have a few short toasts memorized.* A groom at his own wedding banquet was asked to propose a toast to the bride. Unprepared, he got to his feet, put his hand on the bride's shoulder, and said, "Ladies and gentlemen, I—I don't know what to say. This thing was forced upon me—"

4. *Check the context of your toast if it is quoted from a known poem or prose work.* Prince Phillip of Great Britain was told the story of the man who toasted him at a banquet with two lines from John Dryden:

> A man so various he seemed to be
> Not one but all mankind's epitome.

Phillip liked the lines and looked up the remaining lines of the poem:

> Stiff in opinions, always in the wrong
> Was everything by starts and nothing long;
> But in the course of revolving moon
> Was chemist, fiddler, statesman and buffoon.

5. *Don't get ahead of yourself.* When Queen Louise of Prussia met the conquering Napoleon, she drank to him:

"To the health and kindness of Napoleon the Great. He has taken our states, and soon will return them to us."

Napoleon bowed and replied, "Do not drink it all, Madame."

6. *Make sure that the toast you are delivering is appropriate to the group at hand.* Bottoms up is inappropriate at the beginning of a boat race.

"The Finger." The gentleman in this '30s era photograph demonstrates the proper position of the pinky while toasting. *(Library of Congress)*

7. *Don't drink with old Saxons.* An Old Saxon toasting custom required that a man draw the sharp edge of his knife across his forehead, letting the blood drip into his wine cup, and then drinking a health to the woman he loved.

SEE ALSO: *SECRETS; Toastmaster.*

Historic

What follows is a small, chronologically displayed museum of special toasts that were tied to a historic place, cause, or event. There have been hundreds more, but these were some of the most important. One should also be aware of the fact that any number of mottos and rallying cries—"Fifty four Forty or Fight!"; "Remember the Alamo!"; "Remember the Maine!"; "Keep 'em flying!"—were also toasts in their time.

Love and wine are the bonds that fasten us all,
The world but for these to confusion would fall,
Were it not for the pleasures of love and good wine,
Mankind, for each trifle their lives would resign;
They'd not value dull life nor could live without
    thinking,
Nor would kings rule the world but for love and
    good drinking.
                —Toast of 1675.

Some delight in fighting Fields,
Nobler transports Bacchus yields,
Fill the bowl I ever said, 'tis better to lie drunk than
    dead.
                —Toast of 1766.

And he that will this health deny,
Down among the dead men let him lie.
—John Dyer,
"Here's a Health to the King,"
18th century.

Here's to the squire who goes on parade,
Here's to the citizen soldier.
Here's to the merchant who fights for his trade,
Whom danger increasingly makes bolder.
  Let mirth appear,
  Every heart cheer,
The toast that I give is to the brave volunteer.
—American Revolution.

Freedom from mobs as well as kings.
—American,
late 18th century.

We mutually pledge to each other our lives, our fortunes, and our sacred honor.
—Thomas Jefferson.

When lifting high the rosy glass,
Each comrade toasts his favorite lass
And to his fond bosom near;
Ah, how can I the nectar sip,
Or Anna's name escape my lip
When Mary is my dear?
—Sailor's toast, 1795.

Stand to your glasses steady,
  And drink to your comrade's eyes:
Here's a cup to the dead already,
  And hurrah for the next that dies.

—Refrain from a long, morose toast with much lore attached to it. Depending on your source, it was a hymn to cholera, the toast of the English dying in the Black Hole of Calcutta in 1758, or a pledge of soldiers during the first Burmese war. It has been attributed to several authors including Alfred Domett and Bartholomew Dowling. During World War I it was used by British and American pilots.

Ladies and Gentlemen, this is the last time I shall drink to your health as a public man. I do it with all sincerity, wishing you all possible happiness.

—George Washington. On March 3, 1797, the day before he retired from office, he gave a dinner for President-elect John Adams at which he raised his glass and gave this toast.

Rum—the greatest undertaker upon earth.

—Early American temperance toast (to be drunk in water).

Ask nothing that is not clearly right, and submit to nothing that is wrong.

—Andrew Jackson's motto, often used as a toast in the 19th century.

May we never have a Fox too cunning nor a Pitt too
deep.

> —English, early 19th cen-
> tury. It refers to Charles
> James Fox and William
> Pitt, the two great politi-
> cal figures.

May blackness of heart, not blackness of face, distinguish the free man from the slave.

> —Early abolitionist senti-
> ment. Appeared first
> in England (1812) but
> was soon embraced by
> Americans who opposed
> slavery.

Up to my lips and down to my hips
The further it goes, the better it gits
Here's peace at home and plenty abroad—
Love your wife and serve the Lord—Drink!
> —Toast of the antebellum South.

Here's to ye, Mr. Lincoln! May you die both late
  and aisy,
And when you lie with the top of each toe turned
  up to the roots of the daisy,
May this be your epitaph nately writ:
"Tho' traitors abused him vilely,
He was honest and koind, and loved a joke,
And he pardoned Miles O'Riley."
> —Miles O'Riley.

I drink to all, whate'er their creed,
  Their country, rank, communion,
Who in the cause of Freedom bleed,
  And combat for the Union!
> —Union toast.

There are bonds of all sorts in this world of ours,
  Letters of friendship and ties of flowers,
    And true lovers' knots I ween;

Liberation. Toasting the liberation of Paris, August 2, 1944. *(U.S. Army)*

The girl and boy and bound by a kiss,
But there's never a bond, old friend like this:
We have drunk from the same canteen!

—General Charles G. Halpine. This toast was very popular among the Union veterans of the Grand Army of the Republic.

Under the sod and the dew,
  Waiting the judgment day;
Love and tears for the blue,
  Tears and love for the gray.
                —Francis M. Finch.

Nine times nine cheers!
                        —19th-century English
                        toast often directed at
                        Queen Victoria. Over
                        time, it became short-
                        ened to "Cheers!"

May the New Year grant you
a clean shirt
a clear conscience
and a ticket to California in your pocket.
                —Irish, 19th century.

Huge and alert, irascible yet strong,
We make our fitful way 'mid right and wrong.
One time we pour out millions to be free,
Then rashly sweep an empire from the sea!
One time we strike the shackles from the slaves,
And then, quiescent, we are ruled by knaves.
Often we rudely break restraining bars,
And confidently reach out toward the stars.

Yet under all there flows a hidden stream
Sprung from the Rock of Freedom, the great dream
Of Washington and Franklin, men of old
Who knew that freedom is not bought with gold.
This is the Land we love, our heritage,
Strange mixture of the gross and fine, yet sage.
And full of promise—destined to be great
Drink to Our Native Land! God Bless the State!
                —Robert Bridges,
                    "A Toast to Our Native Land,"
                    late 19th century.

A mighty nation mourns thee yet;
Thy gallant crew—their awful fate;

And justice points her finger straight,
Lest we forget—lest we forget!
    —On the sinking of the *Maine.*

Home, boys, home! It's home we ought to be!
Home, boys, home! In God's country;
Where the ash and the oak and weeping willow tree
And the grass grows green in North Ameriky!
    —Toast of the U.S. Army in the Philippines
      at the end of the Spanish-American War.

Their arms our sure defense,
Our arms, their recompense.
  Fall in!
          —Women's toast to men
           returning from the Span-
           ish-American War.

Here's to the Trusts which are not dead as yet,
For the longer you curse 'em the stronger they get.
So if we would strangle their dragon-like breath
Let's try a new method and bless 'em to death.
          —Wallace Irwin, 1904.

To all who put their trust in God— but never their God
in a Trust.

A glass of good Nature's Ale—May its recipe never fail.
      —Water toast of the an-
        tisaloon forces, early
        20th century. "Nature's
        Ale," of course, refers to
        water as does the synon-
        ymous "Adam's Ale."

Ireland—St. Patrick destroyed its creeping things of
other days—may his disciples speedily exterminate the
political reptiles of the present age.
         —Irish, early 20th century.

I've burnt the midnight oil, many knotty problems
  solving;

Allies. Soviet colonel toasting the Americans in Germany, May, 1945. *(U.S. Army)*

I've ponder'd o'er human woes, including those
  involving
The rights of lovely women, to which they cling like
  leeches;
But, tell me, (for I'm all at sea,
As to what the moral teaches)—
When the dears go out to vote, are they to wear our
  breeches?

> —Paul Lowe,
>   antisuffragette toast, 1910.

See our glorious banner waving,
  Hear the bugle call;
Rally comrades to the standard
  Down with alcohol!
        —Nonalcoholic toast, U.S. Popular
          among temperance groups, c. 1915.

To our women, our horses, and the men who ride them.
    —Cavalry toast, World War I. From the French.

To the automobile; the rich man's wine and the poor
man's chaser.

Here's to my car and your car, and may they never
meet.

SEE ALSO: *Alliterative; America; Military; Prohibition; SE-CRETS; Temperant.*

HERE'S TO YOU, AND YOUR FAMILY.

BAKER & TASKER,

❧TAILORS❧

and Dealers in

READY MADE

❧CLOTHING,❧

HATS, CAPS

& GENTS' FURNISHING GOODS.

ODD FELLOWS BLOCK,

Hillsboro' Bridge, N. H.

Home

God bless our mortgaged home.

Here's to home, the place where we are treated best, and grumble the most.

—From an old postcard.

May blessings be upon your house,
Your roof and hearth and walls;
May there be lights to welcome you
When evening's shadow falls—
The love that like a guiding star
Still signals when you roam;
A book, a friend—these be the things
That make a house a home.
—Myrtle Reed,
a house blessing.

SEE ALSO: *General; Guests; Hosts/Hostesses.*

Hosts/Hostesses

A toast to our host
    And a song from the short and tall of us,
May he live to be
    The guest of all of us!

Here's a health to thine and thee,
not forgetting mine and me.
When thine and thee again meet mine and me,
may mine and me have as much welcome for thine
    and thee
as thine and thee have had for mine and me tonight.
                                    —Irish.

Here's to my hostess and host
Jolly good health in this toast
May your journey be good
On the road that you choose
Though it be fast or slow
And Joy attend you all the way
Whichever road you go.

Here's to our hostess, considerate and sweet;
Her wit is endless, but when do we eat?

The Last Performance. Group toast from the 1927 silent film epic. *(MOMA/Film Stills Archive)*

I thank you for your welcome, which was cordial,
And your cordial, which is welcome.

Let's drink to the maker of the feast, our friend and host. May his generous heart, like his good wine, only grow mellower with the years.

May the roof above us never fall in, and may we friends gathered below never fall out.

—Irish.

May you be Hung, Drawn and Quartered!
Yes—Hung with diamonds,
Drawn in a coach and four,
And quartered in the best houses in the land.

To our host,
An excellent man;
For is not a man
Fairly judged by the
Company he keeps?

To the sun that warmed the vineyard,
    To the juice that turned to wine,
To the host that cracked the bottle,
    And made it yours and mine.

To our hostess! She's a gem. We love her, God bless her.
And the devil take her husband.

To our host:
The rapturous, wild, and ineffable pleasure
of drinking at somebody else's expense.
                    —Henry Sambrooke Leigh.

What's a table richly spread
Without a woman at its head?

SEE ALSO: *Friendship; General; Guests.*

Husbands

Here's to a man who loves his wife,
  And loves his wife alone.
For many a man loves another man's wife,
  When he ought to be loving his own.

The Thin Man. William Powell and Myrna Loy from the mystery classic. *(Museum of Modern Art/Film Stills Archive)*

May your life be long and sunny
And your husband fat and funny.

To my husband—may he never be tight; but tight or
sober, my husband.

SEE ALSO: *Alliterative; Anniversaries; Man/Men; Weddings.*

International

An assembly of short toasts to get you through a United Nations reception.

Albanian: Gëzuar.
Arabian: Bismillah. Fi schettak.
Armenian: Genatzt.
Austrian: Prosit.
Belgian: Op uw gezonheid.
Bohemian: Naz dar.
Brazilian: Saúde. Viva.
Chinese: Nien nien nu e. Kong chien. Kan bei. Yum sen. Wen lie.
Czechoslovakian: Na Zdravi. Nazdar.
Danish: Skål.
Dutch: Proost. Geluch.
Egyptian: Fee sihetak.
Esperanto: Je zia sano.
Estonian: Tervist.
Finnish: Kippis. Maljanne.
French: A votre santé. Santé.
German: Prosit. Auf ihr wohl.
Greek: Eis Igian.
Greenlandic: Kasûgta.

Wine Label. From a 19th-century bottle of Italian wine. *(Warshaw Collection, the Smithsonian)*

Hawaiian: Okole maluna. Hauoli maoli oe. Meli kalikama.
Hungarian: Kedves egeszsegere.
Icelandic: Santanka nu.
Indian: Jaikind. Aanand.
Indonesian: Selamat.
Iranian: Besalmati. Shemoh.
Italian: A la salute. Salute. Cin cin.
Japanese: Kampai. Banzai.
Korean: Kong gang ul wi ha yo.
Lithuanian: I sveikas.
Malayan: Slamat minum.
Mexican: Salud.
Moroccan: Saha wa'afiab.
New Zealand: Kia ora.
Norwegian: Skål.
Pakistani: Zanda bashi.
Philippine: Mabuhay.
Polish: Na zdrowie. Vivat.
Portuguese: A sua saúde.
Romanian: Noroc. Pentru sanatatea dunneavoastra.
Russian: Na zdorovia.
Spanish: Salud.
Swedish: Skål.
Thai: Sawasdi.
Turkish: Şerefe.
Ukranian: Boovatje zdorovi.
Welsh: Iechyd da.
Yugoslavian: Zivio.
Zulu: Oogy wawa.

SEE ALSO: *Irish; Latin; Scotch.*

Irish

There is no area of the world where English is spoken
—and probably none where any other language is
spoken for that matter—that can compare to Ireland as
a stronghold for the custom of toasting. More often
than not, toasts go by the name of "blessings" in Ireland. There are large numbers of them, and their use
seems to be on the increase. John B. Keane in a recent
article on the subject said, "Nothing has the grace or
the beauty of an old Irish blessing and recently I was
delighted to learn that instead of dying out, Irish blessings are on the increase. All you have to do is listen and
if you spend a day in the Irish countryside you will go
away with countless blessings ringing in your ears."

Blessings are often used beyond the reach of a glass,
but all make appropriate toasts. A graveside blessing—
"That the devil mightn't hear of his death, 'till he's safe
inside the walls of heaven"—can be equally appropriate as a toast to the departed.

The vast majority of toasts in this section (along with
others scattered throughout the rest of the book) come
from the collection of Jack McGowan of the Irish Distillers International of Dublin, who has pulled them
together from all over his nation.

One other thing. Many Irish toasts are one-liners that lend themselves to being assembled into longer toasts. This is especially true of the many *"May you's."*

A goose in your garden except on Christmas day.

Health and long life to you.
The wife/husband of your choice to you.
A child every year to you.
Land without rent to you.
And may you be half-an-hour in heaven
before the devil knows you're dead.
Sláinte! [Pronounced *slawn-cheh;* it means Health!]

May the frost never afflict your spuds.
May the outside leaves of your cabbage
always be free from worms.
May the crows never pick your haystack
and may your donkey always be in foal.

(For the bachelor) May you have nicer legs than yours under the table before the new spuds are up.

Health to Everyone
From the tip of the roof to the side of the fire
From wall to wall
And if there's anyone *in* the wall, speak up!

Here's a health to your enemies' enemies!

Here's that ye may never die nor be kilt till ye break your bones over a bushel of glory.

Here's to a fair price on a fair day.

Here's to eyes in your head and none in your spuds!

Here's to health, peace, and prosperity;
May the flower of love never be nipped by the frost of disappointment, nor shadow of grief fall among a member of this circle.

Here's to the land of the shamrock so green,
Here's to each lad and his darling colleen,
Here's to the ones we love dearest and most,
And may God save old Ireland—that's an Irishman's toast.

Toastmaster. Jack McGowan of Dublin toasting in Irish whiskey. He is the leading authority on and collector of Irish toasts.

Here's to your health
May God bring you luck
And may your journey be smooth and happy.

May meat always sweeten your pot.

May the day keep fine for you.

May the devil say a prayer for you.

May the enemies of Ireland never meet a friend.

May the horns of your cattle touch heaven.

May the path to hell grow green
For lack of travelers.

May the road rise to meet you.
May the wind be always at your back,
the sun shine warm upon your face,
the rain fall soft upon your fields,
and until we meet again
may God hold you in the hollow of His hand.

May the rocks in your field turn to gold.

May the saints protect you,
And sorrow neglect you,
And bad luck to the one
That doesn't respect you.

May the ship that took your sons away
to farm the Californias
bring home a harvest of riches for Christmas.

May the sun shine warm upon your face and the rains
fall soft upon your fields.

May the swallows be first in your eaves.
May your milk never turn.
May your horses never stray.
May your hens always lay.
May lean bacon hang from your rafters.

May the thatch on your house
be as strong as the thatch on your head;
May the moon be as full as your glass
   and American dollars arrive in the post by
   Christmas.

May there always be work for your hands to do.
May your purse always hold a coin or two.
May the sun always shine on your windowpane.
May a rainbow be certain to follow each rain.
May the hand of a friend always be near you.
May God fill your heart with gladness to cheer you.

May time never turn your head gray.

May we all be alive this time in twelve months.

May what goes down, not come back up again.

May you always wear silk.

May you be seven times better off a year from now.

May you die in bed at ninety-five years,
shot by a jealous husband/wife.

May you look back on the past
with as much pleasure
as you look forward to the future.

May you never give cherries to pigs
or advice to a fool
nor praise the green corn
till you've seen the ripe field.

May you never have to eat your hat.

May you never make an enemy
when you could make a friend
unless you meet a fox among your chickens.

May your fire be as warm as the weather is cold.

May your fire never go out.

May your shadow never grow less.

May your well never run dry.

No wasps near your honey, but bees in your hive.

That a doctor might never earn a dollar out of you
and that your heart might never give out.
That the ten toes of your feet might always steer
   you
clear of misfortune, and I hope,
before you're much older,
that you'll hear much better toasts than this.
Sláinte!

The Irish Heart—Quick and strong in its generous im-
pulses, firm in its attachments, sound to the core.

To a full moon on a dark night
And the road downhill all the way to your door.

To a warm bed, a dry stook, and glass in your window.

To the thirst that is yet to come.

To the three skills of a hare
sharp turning
high jumping
and strong running against the hill.

To twenty years a growing
twenty years at rest
twenty years declining

and twenty years when it doesn't matter
whether we're there or not.

To warm words on a cold day.

Wert thou all that I wish thee,
Great, glorious and free,
First flower of the earth,
And first gem of the sea.
                    —Tom Moore.

Your Health! May we have one together in ten years
time and a few in between.

SEE ALSO: *Babies/Children; Birthdays; Bulls; Christmas; Death;
Food; Health; Historic; Hosts/Hostesses; New Years; St. Patrick's
Day; Weddings.*

OPPOSITE PAGE
New Year's Greeting. An old postcard. *(Author's collection)*

Jewish

The prime Jewish toast is the Hebrew *L'chayim*, which means "to life" or "to your health." *Mazel tov* is also used as a toast. Leo Rosten explains which to use when in his *Joys of Yiddish:* "Some innocents confuse *L'chayim* with *mazel tov,* using one when the other would be appropriate. There is no reason to err. *L'chayim* is used whenever one would say 'Your health,' 'Cheers!' or (I shudder to say) 'Here's mud in your eye.' *Mazel tov!* is used as 'Congratulations.' "

Latin

Ad finem esto fidelis.   Be faithful to the end.
Amor patriae.   The love of our country.
Dilige amicos.   Love your friends.
Dum vivimus vivamus.   Let us live while we live.
Esto perpetua.   Be thou perpetual.
Propino tibi.   I drink to you.

Libations

A drink, my lass, in a deep clear glass,
Just properly tempered by ice,
And here's to the lips mine have kissed,
And if they were thine, here's twice.

A glass in the hand's worth two on the shelf—
Tipple it down and refresh yourself!

A small glass and thirsty!
Be sure never ask it:
Man might as well serve up
His soup in a basket.
                    —Leigh Hunt.

A toast to any gentleman
So shrewd and diplomatic
Who never—though he's in his cups—
Decides he's operatic!

At the punch bowl's brink
Let the thirsty think
   What they say in Japan:
"First the man takes a drink,

— 153 —

Then the drink takes a drink,
   Then the drink takes the man!"

Better to pay the tavernkeeper than the druggist.
                                    —Spanish.

Come, friends, come let us drink again,
This liquid from the nectar vine,
For water makes you dumb and stupid,
Learn this from the fishes—
They cannot sing, nor laugh, nor drink
This beaker full of sparkling wine.
                        —Old Dutch song.

Drink and be merry, for our time on earth is short, and
death lasts forever.

Drink and the world drinks with you;
Swear off and you drink alone.

Drink, for you know not
   When you came, nor why,
Drink, for you know not why
   You go, nor whence.
                —Omar Khayyam.

Drink today and drown all sorrow,
You shall perhaps not do't tomorrow
Best while you have it, use your breath;
There is no drinking after death.
                        —Francis Beaumont
                        and John Fletcher,
                        The Blood Brother.

Drink with impunity—
Or anyone who happens to invite you!
                        —Artemus Ward.

Casablanca. Bogart's immortal "Here's looking at you!" *(MOMA/Film Stills Archive.)*

Fill the bumper fair;
  Every drop we sprinkle
O'er the brow of care,
  Smooths away a wrinkle.
            —Tom Moore.

Fill up the goblet, let it swim
In foam, that overlooks the brim;
He that drinks deepest, here's to him.
            —Charles Cotton.

Hath thy ale virtue or thy beer strength, that the tongue
of man may be tickled and his palate pleased in the
morning.
            —Ben Johnson.

He who goes to bed, and goes to bed sober,
Falls as the leaves do, and dies in October;
But he who goes to bed, and does so mellow,
Lives as he ought to, and dies a good fellow.
            —Parody on Beaumont and Fletcher.

Here is a toast to all the toasts,
  As toasted they should be,
Given by paupers, kings, and hosts,
  With much felicity.

It flies o'er mountains, swims the sea,
  Tunnels the earth below,
Spreading conviviality
  Wherever it doth go.

It is not great, nor is it small,
  Is neither far nor near.
A well-considered wish from all,
  "Another bottle here."
            —James Monroe McLean,
            The Book of Wine.

Here's to a temperance supper,
  With water in glasses tall,
And coffee and tea to end with—
  And me not there at all.

Here's to the bottle which holds a store
Of imprisoned joy and laughter!
  Here's to this bottle,
  Many more bottles,
And others to follow after.

Here's to the man who takes the pledge,
Who keeps his word and does not hedge,
Who won't give up and won't give in
Till the last man's out and there's no more gin.

Here's to water, the best of things that man to man
  can bring.
But who am I, that I should have the best of
  everything?

"The Good Wine Tasters." Lithograph by French artist Claude
Thielley (1811–1891). *(The Christian Brothers Collection at the
Wine Museum of San Francisco)*

Let Princes revel at the pump, let peers with ponds
    make free;
But whiskey, wine, and even beer, is good enough
    for me.

Here's to you that makes me wear old clothes;
Here's to you that turns my friends to foes,
But seeing you're so near—here goes!
Here it goes under my nose—
God knows I need it.

Here's may we never drink worse!

Ho, gentlemen! Lift your glasses up,
Each gallant, each swain and lover;
A kiss to the beads that brim in the cup,
A laugh for the foam spilt over.

Honor, love, fame, wealth may desert us, but thirst is
eternal.

I drink no more than a sponge.
            —François Rabelais.

I drink to your health when I'm with you,
I drink to your health when I'm alone,
I drink to your health so often
I'm beginning to worry about my own.

I drink when I have occasion
and sometimes when I have no occasion.
            —Miguel De Cervantes

If all be true as we do think
There are five reasons why we drink:
Good wine, a Friend, or being Dry
Or lest one should be, by and by . . .
Or any other reason why!
    —Henry Aldrich,
        Dean of Christ Church, c. 1620.

In an honest tavern let me die,
Before my lips a brimmer lie,
And angel choirs come down and cry,
"Peace to thy soul, my jolly boy."
—Walter de Mapes.

Kings it makes gods, and meaner creatures, kings.
—Shakespeare,
King Richard III, Act V.

Let schoolmasters puzzle their brain
With grammar and nonsense and learning;
Good liquor, I stoutly maintain,
Gives genius a better discerning.
—Oliver Goldsmith.

"Lips that touch liquor shall never touch mine";
Thus cried the maiden with fervor divine;
But from her statement what must we infer—
They shan't touch her liquor, or shan't touch her?
—Puck,
A Midsummer Night's Dream

May the beam of the glass never destroy the ray of the
mind.

May the bloom of the face never extend to the nose.

May the tears of the tankard afford us relief.

May you ever have lived—
   May you ever have loved—
So that good drink—
   Will never make you think—
You might have done better.

Mingle with the friendly bowl,
The feast of reason and the flow of soul.
                    —Alexander Pope.

Now here's to Addition—
    Another pint, pray!
Then here's to Subtraction—
    Take th' old one away!
Here's Multiplication—
    So double the wine!
And here's to Division—
    That's yours, and this mine!
                    —Wallace Rice

Observe, when Mother Earth is dry,
    She drinks the droppings of the sky,
And then the dewy cordial gives
    To every thirsty plant that lives.

The vapors which at evening sweep
    Are beverage to the swelling deep,
And when the rosy sun appears,
    He drinks the misty ocean's tears.

The moon, too, quaffs her paly stream
    Of lustre from the solar beam;
Then hence with all your sober thinking!
    Since Nature's holy law is drinking,
I'll make the law of Nature mine,
    And pledge the Universe in wine.
                    —Tom Moore,
                        "The Universal Toast."

O Water! Pure, free of pollution
I vainly wished that I dared trust it.
But I've an iron constitution,
And much I fear that water'd rust it.
                    —W.E.P. French.

One drink is plenty;
Two drinks too many,
And three not half enough.
                    —W. Knox Haynes.

One sip of this will bathe the drooping spirits in delight beyond the bliss of dreams.

—John Milton.

One swallow doesn't make a summer, but it breaks a New Year's resolution.

Take the glass away:—
  I know I hadn't oughter:—
I'll take a pledge—I will—
  I never will drink water.
      —W.E.P. French

The corkscrew—a useful key to unlock the storehouse of wit, the treasury of laughter, the front door of fellowship, and the gate of pleasant folly.

—W.E.P. French.

The first glass for myself, the second for my friends;
  the third for good humor, and the fourth for mine
  enemies.

—Sir W. Temple.

The Frenchman loves his native wine;
The German loves his beer;
The Englishman loves his 'alf and 'alf,
Because it brings good cheer.
The Irishman loves his "whiskey straight,"
Because it gives him dizziness.
The American has no chance at all,
So he drinks the whole damned business.

The man that isn't jolly after drinking
Is just a driveling idiot, to my thinking.
      —Euripides.

Then fill the cup, fill high! fill high!
  Nor spare the rosy wine,
If death be in the cup, we'll die—
  Such death would be divine.
      —James Russell Lowell.

"There here goes another," says he, "to make sure,
For there's luck in odd number," says Rory O'More.
                                        —Samuel Lover.

There are several reasons for drinking,
And one has just entered my head;
If a man cannot drink when he's living
How the hell can he drink when he's dead?

There's naught, no doubt, so much the spirit calms as
rum and true religion.
                                        —Lord Byron.

They that drink deepest live longest.

'Tis a pity wine should be so deleterious,
For tea and coffee leave us much more serious.
                                        —Lord Byron.

Too much is plenty.

                                        —Weber and Fields.

When friends with other friends contrive
To make their glasses clink,
Then not one sense of all the five
Is absent from a drink.
For touch and taste and smell and sight
Evolve in pleasant round,
And when the flowing cups unite
We thrill to sense of sound.
Folly to look on wine? Oh, fie
On what teetotalers think . . .
There's always five good reasons why
Good fellows like to drink.
                        —"A Toast for Toasters"
                            found in a 1937 bar
                            guide and attributed to
                            "E.B.A."

To the cocktail party where olives are speared and
friends stabbed.

Within this goblet, rich and deep,
I cradle all my woes to sleep.
                    —Tom Moore.

SEE ALSO: *Beer/Ale; Biblical; Champagne; Mornings After; Prohibition; Revelry; Spirits; Wine.*

Limericks

There is an old tradition among those who collect limericks of using them as toasts. All limericks work, and all that one has to do is change the original first few words to "Here's to . . ." For example:

Here's to the young lady from Oak Knoll
Who thought it exceedingly droll
At a masquerade ball
Wearing nothing at all
To back in as a Parker House roll.

Love

A Book of Verses underneath the Bough,
A Jug of Wine, a Loaf of Bread—and Thou
   Beside me singing in the Wilderness—
Oh, Wilderness were Paradise enow!
                    —Omar Khayyam,
                       from the *Rubáiyát*

Because I love you truly,
Because you love me, too,
My very greatest happiness
Is sharing life with you.

Brew me a cup for a winter's night.
For the wind howls loud and the furies fight;
Spice it with love and stir it with care,
And I'll toast your bright eyes, my sweetheart fair.
                    —Minna Thomas Antrim

Come in the evening, or come in the morning,
Come when you are looked for, or come without
   warning,

A thousand welcomes you will find here before you,
And the oftener you come here the more I'll adore
  you.

—Irish.

Here's a health to the future,
  A sigh for the past,
We can love and remember
  And love to the last.

Here's to Dan Cupid, the little squirt,
He's lost his pants, he's lost his shirt,
He's lost most everything but his aim,
Which shows that love is a losing game.

Love Affair. Charles Boyer and Irene Dunne from the 1939 film.
(MOMA/Film Stills Archive)

Here's to fertility—the toast of agriculture and the bane of love.

Here's to love and unity,
Dark corners and opportunity.

Here's to Love, that begins with a fever and ends with a yawn.

Here's to love—with its billets doux, bills and coos, biliousness, bills, and bills of divorcement.

Here's to one and only one,
    And may that one be he
Who loves but one and only one,
    And may that one be me.

Here's to the land we love and the love we land.

Here's to the maid who is thrifty,
And knows it is folly to yearn,
And picks out a lover of fifty,
Because he has money to burn.

Here's to the pictures on my desk. May they never meet.

Here's to the prettiest, here's to the wittiest,
Here's to the truest of all who are true,
Here's to the neatest one, here's to the sweetest one,
Here's to them all in one—here's to you.

Here's to the wings of love—
    May they never moult a feather;
Till my big boots and your little shoes
    Are under the bed together.

Here's to the woman that I love,
And here's to the woman that loves me,
And here's to all those that love her that I love,
And to those that love her that love me.

Here's to this water,
  Wishing it were wine,
Here's to you, my darling,
  Wishing you were mine.

Here's to those who love us,
  And here's to those who don't,
A smile for those who are willing to,
  And a tear for those who won't.

Here's to those who'd love us
  If we only cared;
Here's to those we'd love,
  If we only dared.

Here's to you,
May you live as long as you want to,
May you want to as long as you live.

If I'm asleep when you want to, wake me,
And if I don't want to, make me.
                    —Lovers' toast.
                      The man takes one part,
                      the woman the other.

Here's to you who halves my sorrows and doubles my
joys.

I have known many,
  liked a few,
Loved one—
  Here's to you!

I love you more than yesterday, less than tomorrow.

I would be friends with you and have your love.

If I were I, and you were you, would you?
There are times I would and times I wouldn't,
Times that I could and times I couldn't;
But the times I could and would and I felt game
Are the times I'm with you, dear.

It warms me, it charms me,
To mention but her name,
It heats me, it beats me,
And sets me a' on flame.
                    —Robert Burns.

Kisses warm, kisses cold,
Kisses timid, kisses bold,
Kisses joyful, kisses sad,
Kisses good, kisses bad,
Here's to kisses new and old,
Pass the bowl ere I go mad.

Let us be gay while we may
And seize love with laughter
I'll be true as long as you
But not for a moment after.

Let's drink to love,
Which is nothing—
Unless it's divided by two.

Love makes time pass—
Time makes love pass.

May love draw the curtain and friendship the cork.

May those now love
Who never loved before.
May those who've loved
Now love the more.

May we kiss those we please
And please those we kiss.

May we love as long as we live, and live as long as we
love.

Say it with flowers
    Say it with eats,
Say it with kisses,
    Say it with sweets,

Say it with jewelry,
  Say it with drink,
But always be careful
  Not to say it with ink.

Thou hast no faults, or I no faults can spy;
Thou art all beauty, or all blindness I.

To each man's best and truest love—unless it be
  himself.

To every lovely lady bright,
I wish a gallant faithful knight;
To every faithful lover, too,
I wish a trusting lady true.
            —Sir Walter Scott.

The love you give away is the only love you keep.
            —Elbert Hubbard.

They say there's microbes in a kiss,
This rumor is most rife,
Come lady dear, and make of me an invalid for life.

We'll drink to love, love, the one irresistible force that
annihilates distance, caste, prejudice and principles.
Love, the pastime of the Occident, the passion of the
East. Love, that stealeth upon us like a thief in the
night, robbing us of rest, but bestowing in its place a
gift more precious than the sweetest sleep. Love is the
burden of my toast—Here's looking at you.

Were't the last drop in the well,
  As I gasped upon the brink,
Ere my fainting spirit fell,
  'Tis to thee I would drink.
            —Lord Byron.

Yesterday's yesterday while to-day's here;
To-day is to-day till tomorrow appear;
To-morrow's to-morrow until to-day's past—
And kisses are kisses as long as they last.
                              —Oliver Herford.

SEE ALSO: *Alliterative; Anniversary; Celia's Toast; General; Lust;
Wedding.*

Luck

A jolly good smoke, a nicely turned joke,
A handful of trumps when at play;
A drop of old wine, champagne that's fine,
And a run of good luck from today.

As you slide down the bannister of life
May the splinters never face the wrong way.

Everything of fortune but her instability.

Good luck till we are tired of it.

I give you play days, heydays, and pay days!

May Dame Fortune ever smile on you;
    But never her daughter—
    Miss Fortune.

May we ever be able to part with our troubles to advantage.

May your luck be like the capital of Ireland, "Always Dublin."

May your luck ever spread, like jelly on bread.

Stately galleons there are,
   Laden deep with yellow gold;
Treasure argosies from far,
   Jewelled riches in their hold;
May they find a lucky star,
   Captains staunch, and sailors bold,
Not a storm or shoal to bar,
   Not a blast of chill or cold
Till safe harbor they shall win—
Thus may all your ships come in!
            —Oliver Marble.

Then welcome, stranger, cheer be thine.
If thou art a friend, of a friend of mine,
Here's luck. . . .
         —James Monroe McLean,
         The Book of Wine.

To my friend—Luck 'til the end!

SEE ALSO: *Better Times; Friendship; General; Irish.*

Lust

Here's to Eve—mother of our race;
Who wore a fig leaf in just the right place.
And here's to Adam—daddy of us all;
Who was Johnny-on-the-spot,
When the leaves began to fall.

Here's to lying lips,
Though lying lips are bores,
But lying lips are mighty sweet
When they lie next to yours!

Here's to me.
I finally found what's unbelievable—
A sex-mad maid who's inconceivable.

Here's to the game they call Ten Toes;
It's played all over town.
The girls all play with ten toes up,
The boys with ten toes down.

Here's to the girl of my dreams,
She looks like a million—
And is just as hard to make!

Here's to the girl who lives on the hill,
She won't but her sister will.
So here's to her sister.

Here's to the Hereafter.
If you're not here after
What I'm here after—
You'll be here a long time
After I'm gone.

Here's to the Middlesex,
Here's to the fair sex,
Here's to the middle of the fair sex!

Tom Jones. Albert Finney in the memorable eating and drinking
scene from the 1963 film. *(MOMA/Film Stills Archive)*

Here's to the night I met you.
If I hadn't met you, I wouldn't have let you.
Now that I've let you, I'm glad that I met you.
And I'll let you again, I bet you!

Here's to you and here's to me,
And here's to the girl with the well-shaped knee.
Here's to the man with his hand on her garter;
He hasn't got far yet, but he's a damn good starter.

Here's to you, so sweet and good.
God made you; I wish I could.

Hogamus Higamus
Men are Polygamous
Higamous Hogamus
Women Monogamous.

Today's the day,
Tonight's the night,
We've shot the stork—
So you're all right!

To your genitalia,
May they never jail-a-ya.
      —The University of Texas, 1950s.

SEE ALSO: *Love; Revelry; Special Occasions.*

Man/Men

Here's to man—he is like a coal oil lamp; he is not especially bright; he is often turned down; he generally smokes; and he frequently goes out at night.

Here's to that most provoking man
The man of wisdom deep
Who never talks when he takes his rest
But only smiles in his sleep.

Here's to the man that kisses his wife
And kisses his wife alone.
For there's many a man kisses another man's wife
When he ought to be kissing his own.

And here's to the man who kisses his child
And kisses his child alone.
For there's many a man kisses another man's child
When he thinks he is kissing his own.

Here's to the men of all classes
Who through lasses and glasses
Will make themselves asses!

Here's to you, Mister,

"The Flemish Wine Drinker." Line drawing by Pierre Chenu (1730–1800). *(The Christian Brothers Collection at the Wine Museum of San Francisco)*

Whoever you may be.
For you're just the man of the evening,
And nothing more to me.

If I drink too much of your liquor,
And should be foolish enough to get tight,
Would you be a perfect gentleman,
And see that I get home all right?

But, if you and your liquor should conquer,
And I fail to stand the test;
Well, here's to your technique, Mister,
I hope it's better than the rest.

I'll drink to the gentleman who I think
Is most entitled to it;
For if anyone ever can drive me to drink
He certainly can do it.

Man is somewhat like a sausage,
Very smooth upon the skin;
But you can never tell exactly
How much hog there is within.

Man is the only animal that laughs, drinks when he is
not thirsty, and makes love at all seasons of the year.
                                        —Voltaire.

Oh, here's to the good, and the bad men, too.
For without them saints would have nothing to do!
Oh, I love them both, and I love them well,
But which I love better, I can never tell.

To the men I've loved
To the men I've kissed
My heartfelt apologies
To the men I've missed!

To Man:
He is mad; he cannot make a worm, and yet he will
    be making gods by dozens.
                —Montaigne.

Women's faults are many,
Men have only two—
Everything they say,
And everything they do.

SEE ALSO: *General; Husbands; Love; Lust; Parents; Weddings.*

Military

The most common American military toast is the army toast "How!" or, sometimes, "Here's how!" It has been in use for more than a hundred years. Several stories of its origin exist: (1) It came from the Sioux "How kola," which was a sign of friendship (and the basis for the caricature Indian who says "How"); (2) It dates to the Boxer Rebellion and the Chinese "Hao!"; (3) It is a spoken symbol for water—H_2O—and whiskey—W—from which the "2" has been dropped.

Traditionally, the navy has stressed a greater variety in its toasts as the following collection shows:

A stout ship, a clear sea, and a far-off coast in stormy weather.

—Navy.

Foes well tarred, and tars well feathered.
—Navy.

Good ships, fair winds, and brave seamen.
—Navy.

Grog, grub, and glory.
—Navy.

Here's to the ships of our navy
And the ladies of our land;
May the first be ever well rigged,
And the latter ever well manned.
                    —Navy.

I give you muscles of steel, nerves of iron,
tongues of silver, hearts of gold, necks of
leather—the Marines.

Invincible in peace; invisible in war.
          —"To the Militia."

Lots of beef and oceans of grog.
          —Navy.

May no son of the ocean be devoured by his mother.
                    —Navy.

May rudders govern, and ships obey.
                    —Navy.

Put out the red flag, and take ammunition on board.
          —Rear Admiral Robley D. Evans.

Martial Toast. A vintage champagne label. *(Warshaw Collection, the Smithsonian)*

Put your trust in God, boys, and keep your powder dry.
—Colonel Blacker.

Some wine, ho!
And let me the canakin clink, clink;
And let me the canakin clink:
A soldier's a man,
A life's but a span;
Why then, let a soldier drink.
—Shakespeare,
Othello, Act III.

The three generals in peace: General Peace, General Plenty, and General Satisfaction.

—Army.

To long lives and short wars!
—Col. Potter,
M*A*S*H episode,
February 4, 1980.

The wind that blows, the ship that goes, and the lass that loves a sailor.

—Navy.

To our noble commander,
To his honor and wealth:
May he drown and be damned
That refuses the health!
—From an old naval ballad.

True hearts and sound bottoms.
—Navy.

SEE ALSO: *America; Historic.*

To France. GI and friends after the liberation of Paris, August, 1944. *(U.S. Army)*

Mornings After

"A wet night maketh a dry morning,"
Quoth Hendyng, "rede ye right;
  And the cure most fair is the self-same hair
  Of the dog that gave the bite."
                    —"Punderson."

Here's to the good time I must have had!

I wish that my room had a floor
I don't care so much for a door
But this walking around
Without touching the ground
Is getting to be quite a bore.
                    —Gelett Burgess.

If you'd know when you've enough
Of the punch and the claret cup
  It's time you quit the blessed stuff
When you fall down and can't get up.

Lord, how my head aches! What a head have I!
It beats as it would fall in twenty pieces.
                    —Shakespeare,
                      Romeo and Juliet.

Not drunk is he who from the floor
Can rise again and drink some more;
But drunk is he who prostrate lies,
And who can neither drink nor rise.
                    —Eugene Field.

See the wine in the bowl, how it sparkles tonight.
Tell us what can compete with that red sea of light
Which breathes forth a perfume that deadens all
    sorrow,
And leaves us blessed now, with a headache
    tomorrow?
                    —Dr. Doran.

Sing a song of sick gents,
Pockets full of rye,
Four and twenty highballs,
We wish that we might die.

The cocktail is a pleasant drink,
It's mild and harmless, I don't think!
    When you've had one, you call for two,
    And then you don't care what you do!
Last night I hoisted twenty-three
Of these arrangements into me;
My wealth increased, I swelled with pride;
I was pickled, primed, and ossified.
    R-e-m-o-r-s-e!
    Those dry martinis were too much for me.
    Last night at twelve I felt immense;
    To-day I feel like thirty cents.
At four I sought my whirling bed,
At eight I woke with such a head!
It is no time for mirth or laughter—
The cold, gray dawn of the morning after.
            —George Ade,
                from his poem "R-E-M-O-R-S-E."

SEE ALSO: *SECRETS.*

—— 185 ——

New Years

A song for the old, while its knell is tolled,
    And its parting moments fly!
But a song and a cheer for the glad New Year,
    While we watch the old year die!
                        —George Cooper.

Another year is dawning! Let it be
For better or for worse, another year with thee.

As a cat can look at a king
and the beak of a goose
is no longer than that of a gander,
May we all be as good as the next man
in the New Year.
                        —Irish.

As we start the New Year,
Let's get down on our knees
to thank God we're on our feet.
                        —Irish.

Be at war with your voices, at peace with your neighbors, and let every new year find you a better man.
                        —Benjamin Franklin.

Here's to the bright New Year
  And a fond farewell to the old;
Here's to the things that are yet to come
  And to the memories that we hold.

In the New Year,
may your right hand always be stretched out in friendship, but never in want.

                                              —Irish.

In the year ahead,
May we treat our friends with
  kindness
and our enemies with
  generosity.

May all your troubles during the coming year be as
short as your New Year's resolutions.

May the best of this year be the worst of next.

May the Lord keep you in his hand
and never close his fist too tight on you.
And may the face of every good news
and the back of every bad news be toward us
in the New Year.

                                              —Irish.

May the new year help to make us old.

May the New Year bring summer in its wake.

                                              —Irish.

May the New Year grant you
the eye of a blacksmith on a nail
the good humor of a girl at a dance
the strong hand of a priest on his parish.

                                              —Irish.

May your nets be always full—
your pockets never empty.
May your horse not cast a shoe

To 1907. Group toast at Restaurant Martin at 35th Street and Broadway in New York, which had been the site of the fabled Delmonico's. Taken on December 31, 1906. *(Library of Congress)*

nor the devil look at you
in the coming year.
                    —Irish.

Ring out the old, ring in the new,
Ring happy bells across the snow;
The year is going, let him go.
          —Alfred Lord Tennyson.

Should auld acquaintance be forgot,
    And never brought to min',
Should auld acquaintance be forgot
    And days of auld lang syne.
For auld lang syne, my dear,

For auld lang syne,
We'll tak' a cup o' kindness yet,
  For auld lang syne.

And here's a hand, my trusty fiere,
  And gie's a hand o' thine,
And we'll tak' a right guid willie-waught,
  For auld lang syne.
For auld lang syne, my dear,
  For auld lang syne,
We'll tak' a cup o' kindness yet,
  For auld lang syne.

And surely ye'll be your pint stowpt,
  And surely I'll be mine,
And we'll take' a cup o' kindness yet,
  For auld lang syne.
For auld lang syne, my dear,
  For auld lang syne,
We'll tak' a cup o' kindness yet,
  For auld lang syne.
              —Robert Burns.

The New Year is ringing in,
May he be bringing in
The Good Times we've waited for so long in vain!
Without the demanding
All rise and drink standing,
And so say we all of us again and again.

The Old Man's dead. He was okay, maybe
But here's a health to the brand new baby.
I give you 19____!

To a firm hand for a flighty beast
an old dog for the long road
a kettle of fish for Friday
and a welcome for the New Year.
              —Irish.

Welcome be ye that are here,
Welcome all, and make good cheer,
Welcome all, another year.

Special Section 3

Odd Customs

Many of the older toasting customs are impractical in the context of today's values (such as drinking out of the skull of a fallen enemy), but here are three that you can still get away with.

1.   There have always been drinking games and challenges by which the loser must forfeit a glass—that is, have another drink. The following example comes from the very old English custom of drinking *super negulum* or "on the nail." The drinker must leave just the right amount of beer in his glass so that when it is poured out it just covers his fingernail. If too much or too little comes out, the penalty is to drink another glass.

> Here's a health to Tom Brown,
> Let the glass go round,
> Drink up your ale without shrinking,

Picture Puzzle. An early American rhebus toast. *(Library of Congress)*

Put a print [or pond] on your nail,
And kiss the glass's tail,
And fill it up again without ceasing.

2. The Romans started the custom by which men drank to the health of their women by having a drink for each letter of their names. This has been translated into modern terms:

Three cups to Amy, four to Kate be given,
To Susan five, six Rachel, Bridget seven.

Or, for the opposite sex;

It was not my plan to go on a bender,
But I just left Al for Alexander.

3. An old tavern amusement (with appropriate instructions):

This is my top. [Clink the top edges of the glasses.]
This is my bottom. [Clink the lower edges.]
This is my middle. [Clink the sides together.]
And if you're nice to me,
I'll give you a little. [Pour some of your drink into the other person's glass.]

SEE ALSO: *Glossary; Tongue-Twisters; Ultimate Toasts.*

Old Things

I drink as the fates ordain it.
  Come fill it and have done with rhymes.
Fill up the lovely glass and drain it
  In memory of dear old times.
        —William Makepeace Thackeray.

I love everything that's old—old friends, old times, old
manners, old books, old wine.

                —Oliver Goldsmith.

Old wine is wholesomest, old pippins toothsomest,
Old wood burns brightest, old linen washes whitest,
Old soldiers' sweethearts are surest and old
Lovers are soundest.

                —John Webster.

Old wood to burn, old wine to drink,
old friends to trust,
and old authors to read.
                —Francis Bacon.

Parents

Father. May the love and respect we express toward him make up, at least in part, for the worry and care we have visited upon him.

Here's to the happiest hours of my life—
Spent in the arms of another man's wife:
My mother!

To Life. The first half is ruined by our parents and the second half by our children.

To Mother—may she live long enough to forget what fiends we used to be.

We have toasted our sweethearts,
  Our friends and our wives,
We have toasted each other
  Wishing all merry lives;
Don't frown when I tell you
  This toast beats all others
But drink one more toast, boys—
  A toast to—Our Mothers.

Parting

Friendly may we part and quickly meet again.

Happy are we met, happy have we been,
Happy may we part, and happy meet again.

Here's to good-byes—that they never be spoken!
Here's to friendships—may they never be broken!

May we always part with regret and meet again with pleasure.

Must we part?
Well, if we must—we must—
And in that case
The less said the better.
        —Richard B. Sheridan, *The Critic*, Act II.

The pain of parting is nothing to the joy of meeting again.

                    —Charles Dickens.

'Tis grievous parting with good company.
                    —George Eliot.

True friendship's laws are by this rule express'd:
Welcome the coming, speed the parting guest.
                    —Alexander Pope,
                        The Odyssey of Homer, Book XIII.

SEE ALSO: *Friendship.*

Past, Present, and Future

Don't worry about the future,
   The present is all thou hast,
The future will soon be present,
   And the present will soon be past.

Every day should be passed
As though it were to be our last.

Here's to the present—and to hell with the past!
A health to the future and joy to the last!

May we always look forward with pleasure, and backward with regret.

The cares of the day, old moralists say,
Are quite enough to perplex one;
Then drive today's sorrow away till tomorrow,
And then put it off till the next one.
                              —Charles Dickens.

OPPOSITE PAGE

To Columbus. Souvenir postcard distributed at the Columbian Exposition of 1893. *(Warshaw Collection, the Smithsonian)*

The have-beens, the are-nows—and the may-bes!

This is the best day the world has ever seen.
Tomorrow will be better.
                              —R. A. Campbell.

Then fill the bowl—away with care,
    Our joy shall always last—
Our hopes shall brighten days to come,
    And memory gild the past.
                              —Tom Moore.

SEE ALSO: *Age; Anniversary; Parting; Wedding.*

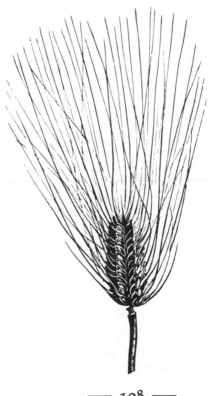

Professional and Occupational

AGRICULTURE

Blessed be Agriculture! If one does not have too much of it.

—Charles Dudley Warner.

Fat cattle, green fields, and many a bushel in your barn.

—Irish.

God speed the plough,
But keep me from the handles!
—Yorkshire toast.

Good luck to the hoof and the horn
Good luck to the flock and the fleece
Good luck to the growers of corn
With blessings of plenty and peace.

May we spring up like vegetables, have turnip-noses, radish cheeks, and carroty hair, and may our hearts never be hard, like those of cabbages, nor may we be rotten at the core.

Some people tell us there ain't no hell,
But they never farmed, so how can they tell?*

To Farmers—founders of civilization.
—Daniel Webster.

BARBERING

He cuts our hair
And shaves our face,
And talks and talks
With ease and grace.

BUSINESS

A man should be honest and upright and true—
    No divvy nor graft nor dishonest intent;
But unless he's a chump who cannot catch on
    He'll find out a way to make thirty percent.
    —M. Quad.

Good trade and well paid.

May the weight of our taxes never bend the back of our credit.

Our mints: The only places that make money without advertising.

Though confidence is very fine,
    And makes the future sunny;
I want no confidence in mine,
    I'd rather have the money.

COOKING

May we always have more occasion for the cook than for the doctor.

---

*This has been adapted to other fields such as mining.

God sends meat, the devil sends cooks.
—Charles VI.

DENTISTRY

'Twould make a suffering mortal grin,
  And laugh away dull care,
If he could see his dentist in
  Another dentist's chair.

To the Dentist:
Who, East, West, North and South,
Always lives from hand to mouth.

FIREFIGHTING

May he never be *toasted* save by the glass of his friends.

Our Fire Department—The army that draws water instead of blood, and thanks instead of tears.

GENERAL

An honest lawyer, a pious divine, and a skillful physician.

May the work that you have
Be the play that you love!
          —E. Geberding.

THE LAW

A bad compromise beats a good lawsuit.

And do as adversaries do in law—
Strive mightily, but eat and drink as friends.
          —Shakespeare,
            The Taming of the Shrew, Act I.

A bumper of good liquor
Will end a contest quicker
Than justice, judge, or vicar;

So fill a cheerful glass,
And let good humor pass.
   —Richard B. Sheridan, *The Duenna*, Act II.

A bumper
To a group of Wranglers from the bar,
Suspending here their mimic war!

A countryman between two lawyers is like a fish between two cats.
                  —Benjamin Franklin.

Fond of doctors, little health;
Fond of lawyers, little wealth.

Here's a toast to a man of great trials and many convictions.

Justice while she winks at crimes,
Stumbles on innocence sometimes.
            —Samuel Butler.

Litigious terms, fat contentions, and flowing fees.
            —John Milton.

May the depths of our potations never cause us to let judgment go by default.

May the judgments of our Benches never be biased.

May we always lie upon our left sides, since the law will not permit us to sleep on our rights.

The glorious uncertainty of the law.

        —First found in Macklin's *Love à la Mode* (1759). Ever since it has been used as a toast at legal dinners.

The Judge:
He populates the city jails
By grave decisions—heads or tails.

The law: It has honored us; may we honor it.
                              —Daniel Webster.

The lawyer—A learned gentleman, who rescues your
estate from your enemies, and keeps it himself.

To Lawyers:
You cannot live without the lawyers, and certainly you
cannot die without them.
                              —Joseph H. Choate.

"Virtue in the middle," said the Devil, as he seated
himself between two lawyers.*

When a festive occasion our spirit unbends
We should never forget the profession's best friends.
So we'll pass round the wine
And a light bumper fill
To the jolly testator who makes his own will.

Who taught me first to litigate,
My neighbor and my brother hate,
And my own rights overrate?
    My lawyer.

Who lied to me about his case,
And said we'd have an easy race,
And did it all with solemn face?
    My client.

MEDICINE

And Nathan, being sick, trusted not in the lord, but
sent for a physician—and Nathan was gathered unto
his fathers.
                              —Old Testament.

---

*This toast sometimes ends with the word "editors."

The doctors are our friends, let's please them well,
For though they kill but slow they are certain.
                              —Beaumont and Fletcher.

To mankind we drink:—'tis a pleasant task:
Heaven bless it and multiply its wealth;
But it is a little too much to ask
That we should drink to its health.

Unto our doctors let us drink,
   Who cure our chills and ills,
No matter what we really think
   About their pills and bills.
                    —Philip McAllister.

When Judgment Day arrives and all
The doctors answer for their sins,
O' think of what they'll get who bring
The howling triplets and the twins.

MINING

May all your labors be in vein.
         —Yorkshire miner's toast.

POLICE

Here's to the policeman who passes our way.
Here's to the mailman who calls every day.
Here's to the babies who continually say:
"Mom, which is my daddy—the blue or the gray?"

POLITICS

Here's to the honest politician—a man who when
bought stays bought.

THE PRESS

The Newspaper—May it fight like an army in the defense of right with strong columns and good leaders.

Beer Garden. Three Maryland politicians imbibing. *(Library of Congress)*

The Press: the great bulwark of our liberties, and may it ever remain unshackled.

—American, 18th century.

The Press: the great corrector of abuses, the shield of the oppressed, and the terror of the oppressor.

We editors may dig and toil
  Till our fingertips are sore,
But some poor fish is sure to say,
  "I've heard that joke before."

PRINTING

The master of all trades: he beats the farmer with his fast "hoe," the carpenter with his "rule," and the mason in "setting up his columns"; he surpasses the lawyer and the doctor in attending to the "cases," and beats the person in the management of the devil.

You can always tell a barber
    By the way he parts his hair;
You can always tell a dentist
    When you're in the dentist's chair;
And even a musician—
    You can tell him by his touch;
You can always tell a printer,
    But you cannot tell him much.

PSYCHIATRY

Here's to my psychiatrist.
He finds you cracked and leaves you broke.

SALES

Here's to us. Never sell a salesman short.

SECURITIES

He keeps us poor all of our lives so we can die rich.

WAITERING

We drink your health, O Waiter!
    And may you be preserved
From old age, gout, or sudden death!—
    At least till supper's served.
                    —Oliver Herford
                    and John Cecil Clay,
                    Happy Days.

WRITING

Authors are judged by strange, capricious rules,
The great ones are thought mad, the small ones
    fools.

The writer's very good health. May he live to be as old
as his jokes!

SEE ALSO: *Special People.*

Prohibition

A dry heaven, and a wet hell;
So it is prohibitors tell;
But who would to a desert go,
When it's nice and wet and soggy
   Down below?

Drink a bottle to us in London
And a stein in old Berlin,
Some rare champagne
If you get to Spain
Is nice to remember us in;
You may drink to our health in Paris
With a flagon of old Cognac,
But if you want the toast
That'll please us the most
Just bring us a bottle back.

Forty miles from whiskey,
   And sixty miles from gin,
I'm leaving this damn country,
   For to live a life of sin.

Four and twenty Yankees,
   feeling very dry,

Imbiber's Guide. Two sides of a Prohibition era mechanical mixer's guide. By moving the cardboard wheel the name and formula for mixed drinks would appear. *(Warshaw Collection, the Smithsonian)*

FORTY FAMOUS COCKTAILS ❦ BEING A COMPENDIUM OF RELIABLE RECIPES CAREFULLY COMPILED FOR USE IN THIS ARID ERA ❦ ENGRAVED WITH HUMBLE APOLOGIES TO THAT MASTER ENGRAVER JOHN HELD JR

Went across the border
  to get a drink of rye,

When the rye was opened,
  the Yanks began to sing
God bless America,
  but God save the King!

—Song/toast popular in Canada
during Prohibition.

God bless America and damn Prohibition.

Here's to Carry Nation,
Of antidrink renown,
Who, though against libation,
Hit ev'ry bar in town!

Here's to Prohibition: May it continue to reduce the
number of men who think they can sing.

Here's to Prohibition,
  The devil take it!
They've stolen our wine,
  So now we make it.

Here's to the "noble experiment's" ignoble death!

Liberty—May it ever be enjoyed by Americans without
prohibition.

May you get through the passport office without de-
tention, through Europe with dissention, and through
customs without detection.

Mother makes brandy from cherries;
Pop distills whiskey and gin;
Sister sells wine from the grapes on our vine
Good grief how the money rolls in.

Ship me somewhere east of Suez,
  where the best is like the worst,
Where there aren't no ten commandments an' a man
  can raise a thirst.
—Rudyard Kipling, used as a "Prohibition Lament."

Thirsty days hath September,
April, June, and November;
All the rest are thirsty too
Except for him who hath home brew.

To my bootlegger: Here's hoping he never has to drink
any of his own.

When Christ turned water into wine
There were no drys to scold and whine;
Today prohibitors would rail
And send the Son of God to jail.

When men were free as a matter of course,
   Millions of dollars in revenue came;
While now millions go, a law to enforce,
   And all but the bootleggers lose at the game.

Wise guys
   Buy supplies;
Dry guys
   Likewise.

SEE ALSO: *Historic; Temperant.*

Speakeasy. A jolly but illegal bar, c. 1928. *(Author's collection)*

Special Section 4

Quotes

Here sleeps in peace a Hampshire Grenadier
Who caught his death by drinking small cold beer,
Soldiers be wise from his untimely fall
And when yere hot drink strong or none at all.
                    —Epitaph on Thomas Thatcher
                      (1764) in Winchester Cathedral.

Here old John Randall lies, who telling of his tale
Lived threescore years and ten, such virtue was in
ale
Ale was his meat, ale was his drink, ale did his heart
revive
And if could have drunk his ale, he still had been
alive.

—Epitaph.

I feel no pain dear mother now,
But Oh I am so dry.
O take me to a brewery
And leave me there to die.
—Anonymous.

In the sixteenth century when there were no Water
Boards, water was really dangerous to drink; everybody in England drank ale, beer and wine. England's
population then was less than the population of London to-day, and the quota of great statesmen, soldiers,
sailors, philosophers, poets and dramatists reared on
beer and wine in those days compares favourably with
the greatness reached in our own sober times.
—A. L. Simons,
Daily Telegraph, April 1931.

This North American has been an inmate of my 'ouse
ove two weeks, yit he hasn't made no attempts to scalp
any member of my family. He hasn't broke no cups or
sassers, or furniture of any kind. (Hear, hear.) I find I
can trust him with lighted candles. He eats his vittles
with a knife and fork. People of this kind should be
encurridged. I purpose is 'elth. (Loud 'plaws.)
—To Artemus Ward, from *Punch,* 1866.

This wine is too good for toast-drinking, my dear. You
don't want to mix emotions up with a wine like that.
You lose the taste.
—Count Mippipoplous to Brett in
The Sun Also Rises, by Ernest
Hemingway.

There must be more beer, cheaper beer, better beer!
People who do not drink beer do not realize that beer
is as important to the working classes as bread. . . . Men
who find they cannot get beer tend to develop a taste
for less innocent liquors. Good ale and good beer are
drinks of temperate men, and it must be confessed that
England has bred a race of mighty fighting men on her
national brew. Good beer is the basis of true temperance.

—*Daily Express,* January 25, 1919.

Who buys good land buys many stones,
Who buys good meat buys many bones,
Who buys good eggs buys many shells,
Who buys good ale buys nothing else.
—Gammer Gurton's Needle.

SEE ALSO: *SECRETS.*

"YOU'LL NEVER MISS THE WATER"

Reunions

Here's a health in homely rhyme
To our oldest classmate, Father Time;
May our last survivor live to be
As bold and as wise and as thorough as he!
     —Oliver Wendell Holmes.

Here's to all of us!
For there's so much good in the worst of us
 And so much bad in the best of us,
That it hardly behooves any of us,
 To talk about the rest of us.

Here's to us that are here, to you that are there, and
 the rest of us everywhere.

Some among many gather again,
A glass to their happiness; friendship,
Amen. . . .
The Survivors.
     —James Monroe McLean,
      The Book of Wine.

Then fill the cup, fill high! fill high!
 Let joy our goblets crown,

Warriors. Fleet Admiral Chester W. Nimitz and General Dwight D. Eisenhower toast one another on the occasion of receiving honorary degrees from Richmond University in 1946. *(Dwight D. Eisenhower Library)*

We'll bung Misfortune's scowling eye,
And knock Foreboding down.
—James Russell Lowell,
from "To the Class of '38."

To friends: As long as we are able
To lift our glasses from the table.

Drinking Scene. One of a set of twelve pencil drawings of imbibers by the 19th-century German artist C. W. Allers. *(The Christian Brothers Collection at the Wine Museum of San Francisco)*

To the good old days . . . we weren't
so good, 'cause we weren't so old!

SEE ALSO: *Colleges and Universities; Friendship; Parting; Past, Present, and Future.*

Revelry

A toast to the fellow
  Who when he drinks deep
Gets royally mellow
  And then falls asleep.
But not to the varlet
  Who as he grows tight,
Turns noisy and scarlet
  And starts in to fight.
          —W.E.S. Fales.

A very merry, dancing, drinking,
Laughing, quaffing and unthinking time.
          —John Dryden.

And the night shall be filled with music,
  And the cares that infest the day
Shall fold their tents like the Arabs,
  And as silently steal away.
          —Henry Wadsworth Longfellow.

But, fill me with the old familiar juice,
Methinks I might recover bye and bye.
          —Omar Khayyam.

Lady with Grapes on Her Head. Advertising card. *(Warshaw Collection, the Smithsonian)*

Care to our coffin adds a nail, no doubt,
And every grain, so merry, draws one out.
                              —Wolcott.

Drink to the girls and drink to their mothers,
Drink to their fathers and to their brothers;
Toast their dear healths as long as you're able,
And dream of their charms while under the table.

Fill up the bowl, upon my soul,
    Your trouble you'll forget, sir;
If it takes more, fill twenty more,
    'Till you have drowned regret, sir.

Fill up the goblet and reach me some,
Drinking makes wise, but dry feasting makes glum.
                              —Oriental.

Gin by pailfuls, wine in rivers,
Dash the window glass to shivers!
            —Sir Walter Scott.

Here is a riddle most abstruse:
    Cans't read the answer right?
Why is it that my tongue grows loose
    Only when I grow tight?

Here, waiter, more wine, let me sit while I'm able,
Till all my companions sink under the table.
                              —Oliver Goldsmith.

Here's pleasure as you like it.

Here's to a guy who is never blue,
Here's to a buddy who is ever true,
Here's to a pal, no matter what the load,
Who never declines, one for the road.

Here's to the love of a beautiful maid
And the love of a staunch true man
And the love of a baby unafraid;
These loves have existed since life began.

But the greatest love, the love of love,
Even greater than that of a mother
Is the tender and passionate, infinite love
Of one drunken sot for another.

Here's to the serpent in the glass—
There's always one in mine;
And when he gets into my legs
I travel serpentine.

I'm tired of drinking toasts
For each small glass of gin.
Let's toss out all the hooey
And toss the liquor in.

In for a high old frolic,
Chiefly alcoholic.

Laugh at all things,
Great and small things,
Sick and well, at sea or shore;
While we are quaffing,
Let's have laughing.
Who the devil cares for more?
                    —Lord Byron.

Let us have wine and women, mirth and laughter
Sermons and soda water the day after.
                    —Lord Byron.

Let us sip and let it slip
    And go which way it will-a
Let us trip and let us ship
    And let us drink our fill-a.

Let's live in haste; use pleasures while we may:
Could life return, 'twould never lose a day.
                    —Robert Herrick.

One glass is wholesome,
Two glasses toothsome,
Three glasses blithesome,

Four glasses fulsome,
Five glasses noisome,
Six glasses quarrelsome,
Seven glasses darksome.
   —After Charles Lamb.

Plus je bois, mieux je chante. (The more I drink, the better I sing.)

There's something I would like to say
   But what I cannot think,
So stand up, comrade, anyway—
   And drink, confound you, drink!

They tell me my love would in time have been
   cloy'd,
And that Beauty's insipid when once 'tis enjoyed;
But in wine I both time and enjoyment defy,
For the longer I drink the more thirsty am I.

Too much work, and no vacation,
Deserves at least a small libation.
So hail! my friends, and raise your glasses;
Work's the curse of the drinking classes.

Toss the pot, toss the pot; let us be merry,
And drink till our cheeks be red as a cherry.
                    —Anonymous, c. 1600.

Turn out more ale, turn up the light;
I will not go to bed tonight.
Of all the foes that man should dread
The first I have had both old and young,
And ale we drank and songs we sung;
Enough you know when this is said,
That, one and all—they died in bed!
          —Webb, Charles Henry , *Dum Vivimus Vigilamus*.

Water, Discretion, and Sleep,
   We may leave to the slaves and the clods.
Wine, Women, and Song we shall keep
   And rest on the knees of the gods.

What would you like to drink to?
To about three in the morning.

Who loves not women, wine, and song,
Remains a fool his whole life long.
                    —John Henry Voss.

SEE ALSO: *Beer/Ale; Champagne; Libations; Lust; Mornings
After; Spirits; Ultimate Toasts; Wine.*

St. Patrick's Day

May the Irish hills caress you.
May her lakes and rivers bless you.
May the luck of the Irish enfold you.
May the blessings of St. Patrick behold you.

May the Leprechauns be near you to spread luck
  along your way
And may all the Irish angels smile upon you on St.
  Pat's Day.

Saint Patrick was a gentleman,
  Who, through strategy and stealth,
Drove all the snakes from Ireland—
  Here's a bumper to his health.
But not too many bumpers,
  Lest we lose ourselves, and then
Forget the good Saint Patrick,
  And see the snakes again.

Success attend St. Patrick's fist,
   For he's a saint so clever;
Oh! he give the snakes and toads a twist,
   He banished them forever.

The anniversary of St. Patrick's day—and may the
Shamrock be green forever.

SEE ALSO: *Irish.*

Scotch

A guid New Year to yin and a'
  And mony may you see,
And may the mouse ne'er run out o'
  Your girnel wi' a tear in its 'e.

Blythe may we a' be,
Ill may we never see!

Here's grand luck, an' muckle fat weans!*

Here's health ta the seeck, an' stilts ta the lame;
Claise ta the back, an' brose ta the wame!†

Here's tae auld Scotland, the land o' our birth,
Wi' its hulls where stormy winds whistle.
Ye can sit for a month on the shamrock an' the rose,
But ye canna sit lang on the thistle!

Here's to them that lo'es us, or lends us a lift.

Here's tae us! Wha's like us?

*Muckle fat weans = big fat children.
†Brose ta the wame = gruel to the belly.

Highlander. *(Library of Congress)*

Da' few and they're deed.
[Here's to us! Who's like us?
Damn few and they're dead.]

May the best ye've ever seen
Be the worst ye'll ever see.

May the mouse ne'er leave our meal pock wi' the tear in its ee.

May the winds o' adversity ne'er blaw open our door.

O, wad some pow'r the giftie gie us
To see oursels as ithers see us!
It wad frae mony a blunder free us.

The deil rock them in the creel that does na' wish us a' weel.

Then let us toast John Barleycorn,
  Each man a glass in hand;
And may his great posterity
  Ne'er fail in old Scotland!

Up wi' yer glesses, an' deil tak the hindmaist!

SEE ALSO: *New Years; Ultimate Toasts.*

Special Section 5

SECRETS

A collection of ancestral information that has been lost to the modern world.

TEN LITTLE-KNOWN BENEFITS OF ALCOHOL.
(From a much longer list appearing in *The Vertuose Boke of Distyllacyon,* 1572.)

1.   It gyveth yonge corage in a person, and cawseth hym to have a good memorye and remembraunce.

2.   It conforeth the harte, and causeth a body to be mery.

3.   It cawseth a good colour in a person whan it is dronke and the hede enoynted therwyth the space of 20 days. . . . It cawseth the here well to growe, and kylleth the lyce and flees.

4.   It cureth Litargiam [lethargy] and all yll humours of the hede.

5.   It heleth the coloure in the face, and all maner of pymples.

6.   In easeth the payn in the teeth, when it is a longe tyme holden in the mouthe, it cawseth a swethe brethe, and heleth the rottyng tethe.

7.   It cawseth the hevy togue to become light and well spekyng.

8.   It drybeth the wyndes out of the body, and is good agaynst the evyll stomake.

9.   It heleth all shronke sinewes, and cawseth them to become softe and right.

10.   It heleth the venymous bytes, and also of a madde dogge, when they wasshed therwith.

EIGHT CONDITIONS OF OVERINDULGENCE.
(From *Pierce Penniless* by Thomas Nashe, 1592.)

The first is Ape drunke, and he leapes, and sings, and, daunceth for the heauens: the second is Lion drunke, and he flings the pots about the house, calls his Hostesse whore, breakes the glasse windowes with his dagger, and is apt to quarrell with any man that speaks to him. The third is Swine drunke, heavy, lumpish and sleepy. The fourth is sheepe drunk, wise in his own conceit, when he cannot bring forth a right word. The fifth is Mawdlin drunk, when a fellow weep for kindness in the middle of his ale, and kiss you saying "By God Captain I love you." The sixth is Martin drunke, when a man is drunke and drinks himself sober ere he stir. The seventh is Goat drunk—with his mind on naught but lechery. The eight is Foxe drunke, when he is craftie drunk, as many of the Dutch men be, will never bargain but when they ave drunk.

SIX WAYS TO PREVENT INTOXICATION.
(From *Valuable Secrets Concerning Arts and Trades,* 1795.)

1. Take white cabbage's, and four pomegranate's juices, two ounces of each, with one of vinegar. Boil all together for some time to the consistence of a syrup. Take one ounce of this before you are going to drink, and drink afterwards as much, and as long, as you please.

2. Eat five or six bitter almonds fasting; this will have the same effect.

3. It is affirmed that if you eat mutton or goat's lungs roasted; cabbage, or any feed; or wormwood, it will absolutely prevent the bad effects which result from the excess of drinking.

4. You may undoubtedly prevent the accidents resulting from hard drinking, if before dinner you eat, in salad, four or five tops of raw cabbages.

5. Take some swallows' beaks, and burn them in a crucible. When perfectly calcined crush them on a stone, and put some of that powder in a glass of wine, and drink it. Whatever wine you may drink to excess afterwards, it will have no effect upon you. The whole body of the swallow, prepared in the same manner, will have the same effect.

6. Pound in a mortar the leaves of a peach-tree, and squeeze the juice of them in a basin. Then, fasting, drink a full glass of that liquor, and take whatever excess of wine you will on that day, you will not be intoxicated.

THREE MONGOL SECRETS FOR TIPPLING.
(From *The Imperial Cookery Book of the Mongol Dynasty.*)

1. Never force yourself to eat, and never get angry, when you are under the influence of drink or you will break out in boils. Washing the face in cold water has the same effect.

2.   Don't ride or jump about, or exert yourself in any way when drunk or you will injure your bones and sinews and undermine your strength.

3.   If you see in your wine the reflection of a person not in your range of vision, don't drink it.

TWO WAYS TO GET DRUNK WITHOUT ENDANGERING YOUR HEALTH.
(From *Valuable Secrets Concerning Arts and Trades,* 1795.)

1.   Infuse some aloe wood, which comes from India, in a glass of wine, and give it to drink. The person who drinks it will soon give signs of his intoxication.

2.   Boil in water some mandrake's bark, to a perfect redness of the water in which it is a-boiling. Of that liquor, if you put in the wine, whoever drinks it will soon be drunk.

TWO WAYS TO REFORM THOSE WHO DRINK TOO MUCH WINE.
(From *Valuable Secrets Concerning Arts and Trades,* 1795.)

1.   Put in a sufficient quantity of wine three or four large eels, which leave there till quite dead. Give that wine to drink to the person you want to reform, and he or she will be so much disgusted of wine, that 'tho they formerly made much use of it, they will now have quite an aversion to it.

2.   Cut in the spring, a branch of vine, in the time when the sap ascends most strongly; and receive in a cup the liquor which runs from that branch. If you mix some of this liquor with wine, and give it to a man already drunk, he will never relish wine afterwards.

TO REFRESH A LARGE NUMBER OF PEOPLE.
(From *Inns, Ales, and Drinking Customs of Old England* by Frederick W. Hackwood, 1909.)

In 1694 Admiral Edward Russell, commanding the Mediterranean fleet, gave a grand entertainment at Alicant. The tables were laid under the shade of orange-trees in four garden walks meeting at a common centre, where there stood a handsome marble fountain. This fountain was converted for the occasion into a gigantic punch-bowl. Four hogsheads of brandy, one pipe of Malaga wine, twenty gallons of lime-juice, twenty-five hundred lemons, thirteen hundred-weight of fine white sugar, five pounds' weight of grated nutmegs, three hundred toasted biscuits, and eight hogsheads of water, formed the ingredients of this monster potation. An elegant canopy placed over the potent liquor prevented waste by evaporation or dilution by rain. To crown this titanic effort, a small boy was placed in a boat expressly built for the purpose, to row round the fountain and assist in ladling the punch into the cups of the six thousand persons who were invited to partake of it.

TO PROPERLY TOAST ANOTHER.
(From *The Irish Hubbub, or the English Hue and Crie* by Barnabe Rich, 1617.)

He that beginnes the health hath prescribed orders; first uncovering his head he takes a full cup in his hand, and settling his countenance with a grave aspect, he crave an audience; silence being once obtained, he begins to breathe out the name peradventure of some honourable personage, that was worthy of a better regard than to have his name polluted at so unfitting a time, amongst a company of drunkards, but his health is drunk to, and he that pledges must likewise off with his cap, kisse his fingers, and bow himself in sign of reverent acceptance. When the leader sees his follower thus prepared, he sups up his breath, turns the bottom of his cup upward and in ostentation of his dexteritie gives the cup a phillip to make it cry *twange,* and thus the first scene is acted.

DRINK FORMULA CALLING FOR ONE (1) COW ALE SYLLABUB.

(18th-century England.)

Place in a large bowl a quart of strong ale or beer, grate into it a little nutmeg, and sweeten it with sugar. Milk the cow rapidly into the bowl, forcing the milk as strongly as possible into the ale, and against the sides of the vessel, to raise a good froth. Let it stand for an hour and will then be fit for use. Cider may be used instead of ale, and the sugar should be proportioned to the taste of the drinker.

Self/Selves

Here's health to my soul and health to my heart;
Where this is going, there's gone many a quart.
Through my teeth and round my gums;
Look out, belly, here it comes!

Here's to ourselves
And wishing all
The wish they wish themselves!

Here's to the health of those we love best—
Our noble selves—God bless us;
None better and many a damn sight worse.
Drink to-day, and drown all sorrow,
You shall, perhaps, not do it to-morrow.
                                   —Beaumont and Fletcher.

Here's to you,
    And here's to me;
But as you're not here,
    Here's two to me.

Our noble selves—may we never be less.

Our noble selves—Why not toast ourselves, and praise

ourselves; since we have the best means of knowing all
the good in ourselves.

Well! Here's luck, great luck,
Such luck as never was known;
May the winner's pockets bulge with coin,
And these pockets be—my own.

Shakespearean

A flock of blessings light upon thy back.
—*Romeo and Juliet,* Act III.

A health, gentlemen,
Let it go round.
—*Henry VIII,* Act I.

Come, come, good wine is a good familiar creature, if
it be well used; exclaim no more against it.
—*Othello,* Act II.

Drink down all unkindness.
—*The Merry Wives of Windsor,* Act I.

Fair thought and happy hours attend on you.
—*The Merchant of Venice,* Act III.

Fill the cup and let it come,
I'll pledge you a mile to the bottom.
—*Henry IV, Part II,* Act III.

Frame your mind to mirth and merriment,
Which bars a thousand harms and lengthens life.
—*The Taming of the Shrew,* Act II.

God's benison go with you; and with those
That would make good of bad, and friends of foes.
                  —*Macbeth,* Act II.

I wish all good befortune you!
          —*The Two Gentlemen of Verona,* Act IV.

I wish you all the joy you can wish.
       —*The Merchant of Venice,* Act III.

Let's drink together friendly, and embrace.
              —*Henry IV, Part II.*

Speak no more of her. Give me a bowl of wine:
In this I bury all unkindness, Cassius.
—Brutus to Cassius, in the tent scene of *Julius Caesar.*

The best of happiness, honor and fortunes keep with
you.
                —*Timon of Athens,* Act I.

To make the coming hour o'erflow with joy,
And pleasure drown the brim.
        —*All's Well That Ends Well,* Act II.

You are welcome, my fair guests; that noble lady,
Our gentleman, that is not freely merry,
Is not my friend: This to confirm my welcome:
And to you all good health.
                —*Henry VIII,* Act I.

You have deserved high commendation, true applause
and love.
                —*As You Like It,* Act I.

SEE ALSO: *Cheese; Food; General; Guests; Military; Professional and Occupational; Wedding.*

Skoaling

Scandinavian toasting hinges for the most part on one word, *skål,* or as it has been anglicized, *skoal.* It is a particular kind of toasting with its own protocol. For starters, one is supposed to engage the eyes of the person toasted and the gaze locked until the act is completed and the glass returned to a point below the neck. One must also know when to skoal. The Swedish Information Service provides these guidelines for anyone planning a formal Swedish dinner or expecting to have to go to Stockholm to pick up his or her Nobel Prize:

Host usually starts by a toast of welcome.
Host then usually drinks with the ladies, one at a time.
Hostess usually begins by drinking with the gentlemen, one at a time.
Guests *do not* toast host or hostess.
Gentlemen toast the ladies, beginning with lady on right, then on left.
Ladies usually do not return the toast.
Gentlemen toast each other.
The older or more prominent person always takes

the initiative; the younger returns the toast before the end of dinner.

Some younger ladies return older ladies' toasts, some don't.

You usually answer a toast in the same wine.

Special Occasions

AFTER A QUARREL

Here's looking at you, though heaven knows it's an effort.

APRIL 15TH

We know it is true that we're wicked,
   That our criminal laws are lax;
But here's to punishment for the man
   Who invented our income tax.

BEFORE AN EXAM

If we must suffer, let us suffer nobly.
                    —Victor Hugo.

COCKTAIL PARTY

To the cocktail party: Where olives are speared and friends stabbed.

CONSCIENCE, MOMENTS OF

Here's to a clear conscience—or a poor memory.

Here's to Conscience. May it waken to hear us toast it and then go to sleep again.

EXPECTANT PARENTS

Here's to one who born will be,
Born of the body, sowed of the soul,
Born of the flesh of you and me.

Out of a love our child will grow. . . .
Greater than light, deeper than dark,
All other love is but a spark.

Here is the toast of the moon and the stars,
To the child . . . who will soon be ours.

FOUR OF US

Here's to the four of us!
Thank God there's no more of us!

or

One bottle for four of us!
Thank God there's no more of us!

THE GRADUATE

A toast to the Graduate—in a class by
himself/herself.

IMPERFECT LOVE

Here's to the man who can bravely say,
"I have loved her all my life—
Since I took her hand on the wedding day
I have only loved my wife!"
Would we not praise him long and well
With the strongest praise that is,
The man who could boldly, firmly tell,
And stick to—a lie like this?

'Tis better to have loved and lost,
Than to marry and be bossed.

You may prate of the virtue of memory,
　Of the days and joys that are past,
But here's to a good forgettery,
　And a friendship that cannot last!

You may talk of a woman's constancy,
　And the love that cannot die,
But here's a health to a woman's coquetry,
　And the pleasure of saying "Good-Bye"!
　　　　　—A written toast left
　　　　　at the Wayside Inn.

INTRODUCTORY

Here's mud in your eyes—while I look
Over your beautiful sweetheart!

JULY 4TH

The Fourth of July—Like oysters, it cannot be enjoyed
without crackers.

LABOR DAY

To Peter J. McGuire, Thank You.

—McGuire was the union
official who in 1882 pro-
posed that the first Mon-
day in September be set
aside as a day for labor
to celebrate its "strength
and esprit de corps."

LATE ARRIVAL

Here's to the Clock!
　Whose hands, we pray heaven,
When we come home at three,
　Have stopped at eleven!
　　　　　—Oliver Herford
　　　　　and John Cecil Clay,
　　　　　Happy Days.

Beer Drinkers. From an ad from the George Wiedmann Brewing Co., Newport, Kentucky, 1904. *(Library of Congress)*

I crept upstairs, my shoes in hand,
  Just as the night took wing,
And saw my wife, four steps above,
  Doing the same damned thing.

Then fill a fair and honest cup, and bear it straight
    to me;
The goblet hallows all it holds, what'er the liquid
    be;
And may the cherubs on its face protect me from
    the sin
That dooms one to those dreadful words,
"My dear, where have you been?"
               —Oliver Wendell Holmes.

LYING

The lie—An abomination unto the Lord, and a very
present help in time of trouble.

NIGHTCAP

In days of old the night-cap
Was worn outside the head:
Let's put ours in the inside,
And then—let's go to bed.
          —W.E.P. French.

May you sleep like a log, but not like a sawmill.

ON THE ROAD

Here's to you and here's to me,
Wherever we may roam;
And here's to the health and happiness
Of the ones who are left at home.

ON THE TRAIL

A health to the man on the trail tonight;
may his grub hold out; may his dogs keep their legs;
may his matches never misfire.
            —Jack London.

OPENING NIGHT

A hit, a very palpable hit.

—Shakespeare, *Hamlet*, Act V.

QUIET EVENING

To the Homely Three:
A good book, a bright light, and an easy chair.

RELIGION

To Church:
The first time one goes he has water thrown on him, the second time he has rice thrown on him, the third time he has dirt thrown on him.

RIOTING, TO THE PREVENTION OF

O' Bacchus who hath sent us wine,
Give us now, we pray,
Wit with drink.
And Thou, Minerva, wisdom send,
That we may abstain from rioting.

RUMORS

Two ears and but a single tongue
    By nature's laws to man belong.
The lesson she would teach is clear,
    Repeat but half of what you hear.

SECOND CHOICE

Here's to you, my dear,
And to the dear that's not here, my dear;
But if the dear that's not here, my dear,
Were here, my dear,
I'd not be drinking to you, my dear.

THREE OF US

I'm as dear to you as he,
He's as dear to me as thee,
You're as dear to him as me,
Here's to "Three's good company."

TROUBLE

Here's to ya,
Here's for ya,
I wish to hell
I never saw ya.

A VERY SPECIAL INTERLUDE

Where is the heart that would not give
Years of drowsy days and nights,
One little hour like this to live—
Full to the brim of life's delight?

—Tom Moore.

Special People

ADAM AND EVE

When Eve, upon the first of men
    The apple pressed with specious cant,
Oh, what a thousand pities, then,
    That Adam was not Adamant.
                            —Thomas Flood.

THE BACHELOR

Here's to single blessedness!

THE BAD SINGER

Swans sing before they die; 'twere no bad thing
Did certain persons die before they sing.

THE BORE

Again I hear that creaking step—
He's rapping at the door!—
Too well I know that boding sound
That ushers in a bore.

I do not tremble when I meet
The stoutest of my foes,
But heaven defend me from the man
Who comes—but never goes.

Society is now one polished horde,
Formed of two mighty tribes—the bores and bored.

The Bore: May he give us a few brilliant flashes of
silence.

THE COWBOY

Here's to luck, and hoping God will take a likin' to us!
—Cowboy, Dakota, c. 1890.

Up to my lips and over my gums;
Look out guts, here she comes.

—Cowboy toast that was
collected by John and
Alan Lomax for their
*Cowboy Songs and Other
Frontier Ballads* (1916 edi-
tion).

CREDITORS

Here's to our creditors—may they be
Endowed with three virtues:
Faith, Hope, and Charity!

Here's to the creditor—
    Long may he waive.

FAT PEOPLE

A toast to us, my good, fat friends,
To bless the things we eat;
For it has been full many a year,
Since we have seen our feet.

Yet who would lose a precious pound,
By trading sweets for sours?
It takes mighty girth indeed,
To hold such hearts as ours!
> —Wallace Irwin,
> "Fat Man's Toast,"
> 1904.

THE FINANCIALLY INDISPOSED

'Tis easy enough to say: "Fill 'em!"
When your bank doesn't say: "Overdrawn."
　But the man worthwhile,
　Is the man who can smile,
When every darned cent is gone.

FOOLS

Let us toast the fools; but for them the rest of us could
not succeed.
> —Samuel L. Clemens.

THE HOBO

To the holidays—all 365 of them.

THE LIAR

May every liar be blessed with a good memory!
> —Samuel L. Clemens.

MISERS

Here's to misers—whose abstinence gives us the more
to drink.

MOTHERS-IN-LAW

Here's to our dear old mother-in-law,
　With all her freaks and capers,
For were it not for dear old ma,
　What would become of the "comic papers"?

Man of Leisure. Unidentified photo. *(Library of Congress)*

OMAR KHAYYAM

Here's to old Omar Khayyam—
  I'm stuck on that beggar—I am!
His women and wine are something divine—
  For his verses I don't care a damn!

RICHARD WAGNER

Here's to you, Richard Wagner,
  With your horns and your bassoons;
What a hit you'd have made in music
  Had you only tackled tunes.

THE SMOKER

It isn't the cough
That carries you off;
It's the coffin
They carry you off in.

THE SPENDER

Lift 'em high and drain 'em dry
To the guy who says, "My turn to buy!"

THE USURER

May you take as much interest in Heaven
As I know you have taken on Earth.

THE VIRGIN

Here's to _____,
For her, life held no terrors
Born a virgin, died a virgin
No hits, no runs, no errors.

SEE ALSO: *Professional and Occupational.*

Spirits
(ardent)

A drop of whiskey
Ain't a bad thing right here!
　　　　—Bret Harte.

A Toast to the Three Great American Birds:
　　May you always have an Eagle in your pocket,
　　A Turkey on your table,
　　And Old Crow in your glass.

Candy is dandy, but liquor is quicker.
　　　　　　—Ogden Nash.

Don't die of love; in Heaven above
　　Or hell, they'll not endure you;
Why look so glum when Doctor Rum
　　Is waiting for to cure you?
　　　　　　　—Oliver Herford.

　Drink rum, drink rum,
Drink rum, by Gum, with me;
　For I don't give a damn
　For any damn man
That won't take a drink with me.

Fifteen men on the Dead Man's Chest—
　　Yo-ho-ho and a bottle of rum!
Drink and the devil had done for the rest—
　　Yo-ho-ho and a bottle of rum!
　　　　　　　—Robert Louis Stevenson,
　　　　　　　Treasure Island.

Here is to Irish, a whiskey with heart,
that's smooth as a Leprechaun's touch,
yet as soft in its taste as a mother's embrace
and a gentleness saying as much.

Here's to the man without a shirt to his back,
May he deck himself out with a dickey;
And here's to the man, who of rums finds a lack,
May he fill himself up with gin rickey.

How beautiful the water is!
To me 'tis wondrous sweet—
For bathing purposes and such;
But liquor's better neat.
　　　　　　　—Mrs. C. O. Smith.

Keep your head cool and your feet warm,
And a glass of good whiskey will do you no harm.

On land or at sea
One need not be wary:
A well made old-fashioned
prevents *beri beri.*

If wine tells truth, and so have said the wise;
It makes me laugh to think how brandy lies.
　　　　　　　—Oliver Wendell Holmes.

Inspiring bold John Barleycorn,
What dangers thou cans't make us scorn
Wi' tippling we fear nae evil
Wi' usquebae we'll face the devil.*
　　　　　　　—Robert Burns,
　　　　　　　"Tam o' Shanter."

---

*Usquebae = whiskey.

"Here's health and strength. Drink St. Raphaël!
Like me,—be hearty, strong and hale."

Lady with Small Glass. Old advertising card. *(Warshaw Collection, the Smithsonian)*

Let those who will, praise fragrant wine,
That slowly brings on dizziness.
  Good whiskey, clear,
  To me is dear,
For two drinks does the business.

May we never be out of spirits.

Rum, rum, Jamaica rum,
Who in thy praise is dumb?
The rich, the poor, the gay, the glum,
All call thee good, Jamaica Rum.
                    —Sir Arthur Sullivan.

This cordial julep here
That flames and dances in its crystal bounds.
                    —John Milton,
                        Comus.

Well, if it isn't gin,
Was meant to do us in,
The chances are it's lemonade or dates.
            —A. P. Herbert in
                Peter Owens's *A History of Gin.*

Whiskey, drink divine,
    Why should drivellers bore us
With the praise of wine
    When we have thee before us?
                —Joseph O'Leary.

SEE ALSO: *Libations; Mornings After; Prohibition; Revelry.*

Sports

It would appear that people who write good toasts tend to fish and play poker rather than, say, hunt and play tennis. As the following toasts seem to illustrate, the great toasters have gotten their exercise from hoisting glasses.

A little whiskey now and then
Is relished by the best of men;
It surely drives away dull care,
And makes ace high look like two pair.

Camp life is just one canned thing after another.
                              —Toast to camping.

Gentlemen, the Queen!
She gazed at us serene,
She filled his flush,
Amidst the hush—
And gathered in the green.

Not the laurel—but the race,
Not the quarry—but the chase;
Not the dice—but the play
May I, Lord, enjoy always!

Poker—Like a glass of beer, you draw to fill.

The hand that rocks the cradle
    Is the hand that rules the earth—
But the hand that folds four aces!
    Bet on it for all you're worth.

There was a man in our town,
    And he was wondrous wise.
He jumped into a tournament
    And came out with a prize.
And when he saw the cup he'd won,
    With all his might and main,
He jumped into ten entry lists
    But never won again.

SEE ALSO: *Fishing.*

Club Dance. Arthur Siegel photograph of a party at the Detroit Yacht Club during the summer of 1940. *(Library of Congress)*

States

CALIFORNIA

In the fold of the grape let's pledge her,
Land favored by luck and fate,
California must be heaven,
For she owns the golden gate.
—W.E.P. French.

To California. Where Earth is here so kind that just
tickle her with a hoe and she laughs with a harvest.
—Ernest Jarrold.

COLORADO

The cattle upon a thousand hills,
And the gold of El Dorado,
All kinds of climate, but darned few ills:
Full glasses—To Colorado!
—W.E.P. French.

KENTUCKY

Kentucky, oh, Kentucky,
How I love your classic shades,

Where flit the fairy figures
Of the star-eyed Southern maids;
Where the butterflies are joying
'Mid the blossoms newly born;
Where the corn is full of kernels,
And the Colonels full of corn!
                    —Will Lampton.

MASSACHUSETTS

Here's to old Massachusetts
The home of the sacred cod
Where the Adamses vote for Douglas
And the Cabots walk with God.
                    —Given at the 25th anniversary dinner
                       of the Harvard class of 1880.

NEW ENGLAND

Where Hubbard squash and huckleberries grow to
    powerful size,
And everything is orthodox from preachers down to
    pies.
                                    —Eugene Field.

NEW JERSEY

The fish's blood is very white,
While ours is red as flame,
The "skeeter" has no blood at all,
But gets there just the same.

NORTH CAROLINA

State of the old north star,
Of turpentine and tar,
    There's nothing finer
On God's green earth than you—
That's why we're drinking to
    North Carolina.
                            —W.E.P. French.

MAINE

Sure, stolen fruit's the sweetest
  Of all the fruit that ever grew,
So, in spite of Prohibition,
  Maine, were going to drink to you.
                    —W.E.P. French.

RHODE ISLAND

There's Minnesota's Gopher,
  And Texas's Lonely Star,
And California's Golden Bear,
  All famed both near and far;
But 'tis not to these I pledge,
  Though all are good, I trow—
I toast old Roger Williams's Farm—
  It's called Rhode Island now!

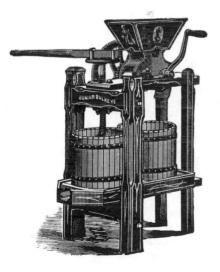

Temperant

A fig then for Burgundy, Claret or Mountain,
  A few scanty glasses must limit your wish.
But here's to the toper that goes to the fountain,
  The drinker that verily "drinks like a fish."
                              —Thomas Hood.

Bacchus has drowned more men than Neptune.

Balm of my cares, sweet solace of my toils!
  Hail juice benignant!
To the unknown beloved,
  This is my good wishes.
                              —Coffee toast.

Black as the devil,
Strong as death,
Sweet as love, and
Hot as hell!
    —Coffee toast.

Cold water: We never want cash to buy it, we are never ashamed to ask for it, and never blush to drink it.

Drinking water neither makes a man sick, nor in debt, nor his wife a widow.

He believes in drinking quantities of water
Undiluted by the essence of the grape.
                    —Harry Graham.

Here's to wine—safer outside than in.

I have found water everywhere that I have travelled
. . . and everywhere water has been my beverage.
                    —Thomas Cook,
                    founder of the
                    international tour
                    company.

If you drink like a fish,
Drink what a fish drinks.

Beastly Toast. Ad from the Tuft's Soda Water exhibit at the Philadelphia Centennial, 1876. *(Warshaw Collection, the Smithsonian)*

It droppeth as the gentle rain from heaven.
—Portia's speech,
from Shakespeare's *The Merchant of Venice*
Act 14 Scene 1

O' Water for me! Bright Water for me,
And wine for the tremulous debauchee.
—*McGuffey's New Eclectic Speaker,* 1858.

Our drink shall be water, bright, sparkling with glee
The gift of our God, and the drink of the free.

There is a devil in every berry of the grape.
—The Koran.

Water—Ever bracing, ever satisfying, ever plenty, and
never mocking.

SEE ALSO: *Historic.*

Thanksgiving

Here's to the blessings of the year,
Here's to the friends we hold so dear,
To peace on earth, both far and near.

Here's to the day when the Yankees first
    acknowledge
Heaven's good gifts with Thank'ees.

To our national birds—
    The American Eagle,
    The Thanksgiving Turkey;
May one give us peace in all our States—
And the other a piece for all our plates.

When turkey's on the table laid,
    And good things I may scan,
I'm thankful that I wasn't made
A vegetarian.
                    —Edgar A. Guest.

Toastmaster

Three toasts for the person who hardly ever gets toasted, along with a set of axioms that should prove useful if you are ever called on to perform this duty.

An ambidextrous man is he;
  Watch closely, and you'll understand,
A wonder in his way—you see,
  He can toastmast with either hand.

Every rose has its thorn,
  There's fuzz on all the peaches;
There never was a dinner yet
  Without some lengthy speeches.

We'll bless our toastmaster,
Wherever he may roam,
If he'll only cut the speeches short
And let us all go home.

TOASTMASTER'S AXIOMS

1.   The toastmaster should not be the whole thing.

Banqueteer. From a series of twelve pencil drawings by the German artist C. W. Allers. *(The Christian Brothers Collection at the Wine Museum of San Francisco)*

2.   The toastmaster should allow the respondents a little of the time set apart for the speaking.

3.   The toastmaster should under no circumstances deliver the respondent's speech in introducing him.

4.   The toastmaster should not tell every known story in introducing the speakers. Leave a few for them to tell.

5.   The toastmaster should not, after a speaker has concluded his speech, express his approval by making the speech over again or trying to improve on it.

6.   The toastmaster should try to make the speakers feel at home. There are moments when even the most calloused speakers wish they were.

7.   The toastmaster should always have in his repertoire the phrase "We have with us tonight." This not only relieves the apprehension of the audience, but also allows the toastmaster to say an undisputed thing in a solemn way.

8.   The words "needs no introduction" can also be used with effect. Do not, however, follow with a biographical sketch or excerpts from *Who's Who*.

9.   The toastmaster's introduction of a speaker should not, as a rule, be longer than the speech of the respondent.

10.   The toastmaster's introduction, on the other hand, should not be so brief as to be brutal. "The next is Mr. Williams, who will talk to us," is nothing short of criminal.

11.   The toastmaster should be empowered by law to kill a speaker who talks over two hours.

12.   The toastmaster must please everybody and offend nobody.

13.   The toastmaster should have at least a speaking acquaintance with the respondents.

14.   The toastmaster must keep sober.

> —These axioms were found in Arthur Leroy Kaser's *Good Toasts and Funny Stories,* 1923.

SEE ALSO: *Hints for Effective Toasting.*

Tongue-Twisters

A half-dozen traditional toasts that not only express a sentiment but double as sobriety tests.

Here's a health to all those that we love,
Here's a health to all those that love us,
Here's a health to all those that love them that love
   those that love them
that love those that love us.

Here's a health to you and yours who have done such things for us and ours; and when we and ours have it in our powers to do for you and yours what you and yours have done for us and ours, then we and ours will do for you and yours what you and yours have done for ours.

Here's to the girl that I love,
And here's to the girl that loves me,
And here's to all those that love her that I love,
And to those that love her that loves me.

Here's to you two and to we two,
If you two love we two
As we two love you two,

Then here's to we four!
But if you two don't love we two
As we two love you two,
Then here's to we two and no more.

Here's to you,
  Here's two to you,
And two to you two, too,
  And to you two, too, here's two.

Tho' a kiss be a-miss,
She who misses the kisses
As Miss without kiss
May miss being a Mrs.
And he who, a-miss,
Thinks both Missed and Kisses
Will miss Miss and Kiss
And the kisses of Mrs.

Ultimate Toasts

The "ultimate" toast is that in which the toast is made, the drink drained at one gulp, and the glass thrown to the floor, against a wall, or into the fire. They were in style when the Czars ruled Russia, during the days of George III in England when one toasted the king (as no lesser mortal was supposed to be honored from the same glass), and in the great banquet halls of seventeenth- and eighteenth-century Scotland when it was done to this toast:

> Up with it, up with it, up with it!
> Down it, down it, down it!
> From me, from me, from me!
> To me, to me, to me!
> May all your days be good, my friend!
> Take it down!
> And no other shall drink from this glass again
> evermore!

At this point the glass was thrown with gusto over the left shoulder.

Ultimate toasts are now definitely out of style. A pity because they could do a lot to liven up suburban dinner parties. Should you care to try this shattering experience, you will want to follow proper form and place your right foot on your chair and your left on the table.

Weddings

"Health and happiness" and "May all your troubles be little ones" are the most common wedding toasts. They have become clichés. Some options:

A Second Marriage:
To the triumph of hope over experience.
> —Samuel Johnson, 1770.

A toast to love and laughter and happily ever after.

A toast to the groom—and discretion to his bachelor friends.

Down the hatch, to a striking match!

Drink, my buddies, drink with discerning,
Wedlock's a lane where there is no turning;
Never was owl more blind than lover;
Drink and be merry, lads; and think it over.
> —Bachelor party toast.

Grow old with me!
The best is yet to be,
The last of life,

For which, the first is made.
　　　　—Robert Browning.

Here's to *my* mother-in-law's daughter,
　　Here's to *her* father-in-law's son;
And here's to the vows we've just taken,
　　And the life we've just begun.

Here's to the bride and mother-in-law,
Here's to the groom and father-in-law,
Here's to sister and brother-in-law,
Here's to friends and friends-in-law,
May none of them need an attorney-at-law.

Here's to thee and thy folks from me and my folks;
And if thee and thy folks love me and my folks
As much as me and my folks love thee and thy
　　folks,
Then there never was folks since folks was folks
Loved me and my folks as much as thee and thy
　　folks.

Here's to the Bride and the Groom!
　　May you have a happy honeymoon,
May you lead a happy life,
　　May you have a bunch of money soon,
And live without all strife.

Here's to the bride that is to be,
　　Here's to the groom she'll wed,
May all their troubles be light as bubbles
　　Or the feathers that make up their bed!

Here's to the groom with bride so fair,
And here's to the bride with groom so rare!

Here's to the happy man: All the world loves a
　　lover.
　　　　　　　　—Ralph Waldo Emerson.

Here's to the husband—and here's to the wife;
May they remain lovers for life.

I drink to myself and one other,
And may that one other be he
Who drinks to himself and one other,
And may that one other be me.

It is written:
"When children find true love,
parents find true joy."
Here's to your joy and ours,
from this day forward.
                    —Parents' toast.

Let us toast the health of the bride;
    Let us toast the health of the groom,
Let us toast the person that tied;
    Let us toast every guest in the room.

Look down you gods,
And on this couple drop a blessed crown.
                    —Shakespeare.

Love, be true to her; Life, be dear to her;
Health, stay close to her; Joy, draw near to her;
Fortune, find what you can do for her,
Search your treasure-house through and through for
    her,
Follow her footsteps the wide world over—
And keep her husband always her lover.
                    —Anna Lewis,
                        "To the Bride."

Marriage: A community consisting of a master, a mistress and two slaves—making in all, two.
                    —Ambrose Bierce.

Marriage is a wonderful institution, but who wants to live in an institution.
                    —Groucho Marx.

May their joys be as bright as the morning, and their sorrows but shadows that fade in the sunlight of love.

(6) ALIENATION—His Wedding Eve at the Bachelor Club.
Copyright 1901 by Underwood & Underwood

Bachelor Party. From the turn of the century, when such festivities were formal events. *(Author's collection)*

May their joys be as deep as the ocean
And their misfortunes as light as the foam.

May we all live to be present at their Golden
    Wedding.
May you grow old on one pillow.
                              —Armenian.

May you have many children
and may they grow as mature in taste
and healthy in color
and as sought after
as the contents of this glass.

                              —Irish.

May you live forever, may I never die.

May your love be as endless as your wedding rings.

May your wedding days be few and your anniversaries many.

May you have enough happiness to keep you sweet; enough trials to keep you strong; enough sorrow to keep you human; enough hope to keep you happy; enough failure to keep you humble; enough success to keep you eager; enough friends to give you comfort; enough faith and courage in yourself, your business, and your country to banish depression; enough wealth to meet your needs; enough determination to make each day a better day than yesterday.

Needles and pins, needles and pins
When a man marries his trouble begins.

Never above you. Never below you. Always beside you.
                                        —Walter Winchell.

These two, now standing hand in hand,
   Remind us of our native land,
For when today they linked their fates,
   They entered the United States.

To my wife,
My bride and joy.

To the newlyweds: May "for better or worse" be far better than worse.

Wedlock's like wine—not properly judged of till the second glass.
                                        —Ernest Jarrold.

SEE ALSO: *Anniversary; Husbands; Wives.*

Wine

A bottle of good wine, like a good act, shines ever in the retrospect.

        —Robert Louis Stevenson
          in "The Silverado Squatters."

A warm toast.
Good company.
A fine wine.
May you enjoy all three.

Any port in a storm.

Balm of my cares, sweet solace of my toils, Hail juice benignant!

        —Thomas Wharton.

Clean glasses and old corks.

Comrades, pour the wine tonight
For the parting is with dawn;
Oh, the clink of cups together,
With the daylight coming on!
        —Richard Hovey.

— A la santé du raisin!.. puisse-t-il ne pas être malade cette année!

"To the Health of the Grapes." Lithograph by Honoré Daumier (1808–1879). *(The Christian Brothers Collection at the Wine Museum of San Francisco)*

Count not the cups; not therein lies excess
In wine, but in the nature of the drinker.

For of all labors, none transcend
The works that on the brain depend;
Nor could we finish great designs
Without the power of generous wines.

Give of your wine to others,
  Take of their wine to you.
Toast to life, and be toasted awhile,
  That, and the cask is through.
            —James Monroe McLean,
              The Book of Wine.

God, in His goodness, sent the grapes
To cheer both great and small;
Little fools will drink too much,
And great fools none at all.

God made Man,
Frail as a Bubble
God made Love
Love made Trouble
God made the Vine
Was it a sin
That Man made Wine
To drown Trouble in?
    —Oliver Herford,
      The Deb's Dictionary.

Good wine makes good blood;
Good blood causeth good humors;
Good humors cause good thoughts;
Good thoughts bring forth good works;
Good works carry a man to heaven.
Ergo:
Good wine carrieth a man to heaven.
                —James Howell
                  to Lord Clifford.

He that drinks is immortal
For wine still supplies
What age wears away;
How can he be dust
That moistens his clay?
                —H. Purcell.

He who clinks his cup with mine,
Adds a glory to the wine.
                —George Sterling.

Here's a bumper of wine; fill thine, fill mine:
Here's a health to old Noah, who planted the vine!
                            —R. H. Barham.

Here's to mine and here's to thine!
   Now's the time to clink it!
Here's a flagon of old wine,
   And here we are to drink it.
                —Richard Hovey.

Here's to old Adam's crystal ale,
Clear, sparkling and divine,
Fair H_2O, long may you flow,
We drink your health (in wine).
                —Oliver Herford.

Here's to the man who knows enough
To know he's better without the stuff;
Himself without, the wine within,
So come, me hearties, let's begin.

Here's to the man
Who owns the land
That bears the grapes
That makes the wine
That tastes as good
As this does.

Here's to Water, water divine—
   It dews the grapes that give us wine.

I often wonder what the vintners buy
One half so precious as the stuff they sell.
                —Omar Khayyam.

Let those who drink not, but austerely dine, dry up in
law; the Muses smell of wine.
                            —Horace.

Water Toast. Illustrated toast from a book of toasts for members of the Elks. *(Author's collection)*

This bottle's the sun of our table,
  His beams are rosy wine;
We, plants that are not able
  Without his help to shine.

This wine is full of gases
  Which are to me offensive,
It pleases all you asses
  Because it is expensive.
                    —A. P. Herbert.

When I die—the day be far!
Should the potters make a jar
Out of this poor clay of mine,
Let the jar be filled with wine!

When wine enlivens the heart
May friendship surround the table.

Wine and women—May we always have a taste for
both.

  Who was it, I pray,
    On the wedding day
Of the Galilean's daughter
    With a touch divine
    Turned in wine
Six buckets of *filtered* water?
                    —Oliver Wendell Holmes.

Wine improves with age—I like it more the older I get.

SEE ALSO: *Alliterative; Biblical; Celia's Toast; Champagne; General; Libations; Prohibition; Revelry.*

Wives

A good wife and health
Are a man's best wealth.

Here's to the man who takes a wife,
Let him make no mistake:
For it makes a lot of difference
Whose wife it is you take.

To our wives and sweethearts. May they never meet!

Late last night I slew my wife,
Stretched her on the parquet flooring:
I was loath to take her life,
But I had to stop her snoring.

A health to our widows. If they ever marry again may
they do as well!

SEE ALSO: *Anniversaries; Weddings; Woman/Women.*

BAMFORTH & CO.

(HEARTIEST CONGRATULATIONS.)

May your troubles be little ones.

Wedding Card. An old postcard. *(Author's collection)*

Woman/Women

Drink to fair woman, who, I think,
   Is most entitled to it;
For if anything drives men to drink,
   She certainly can do it.

Fill, fill, fill a brimming glass
Each man toast his favorite lass,
He who flinches is an ass,
Unworthy of love or wine.

Here's looking at you, dear!
Though I should pour a sea of wine,
My eyes would thirst for more.

Here's to the gladness of her gladness when she's
   glad,
Here's to the sadness of her sadness when she's sad;
But the gladness of her gladness,
And the sadness of her sadness,
Are not in it with the madness of her madness when
   she's mad.

Here's to the lasses we've loved, my lad,
Here's to the lips we've pressed;

Mademoiselle Yvonne

Demure despite her nudity,
She gazes quite sans crudity
Upon the skulls both thatched and bald
Of patrons who are often called
    Great Gourmets.

She's not the Lady of Shalott,
She's what a wife is often not,
She silent hangs with mellow eye
Watching the world come and go by
    Without Emotion.

She is the ideal of our dreams,
When brain with wine and food careens,
Yet always does she stay quite chaste
And never does she make least haste—
    The Lady of Locke-Ober's! LAWRENCE DAME

"Yvonne." Painting in the Locke-Ober restaurant in Boston.

For of kisses and lasses,
Like liquor in glasses,
   The last is always the best.

I have never studied the art of paying compliments to women, but I must say that if all that has been said by orators and poets since the creation of the world, if praise of women were applied to the women of America, it would not do them justice. God bless the women of America.

—Abraham Lincoln.

Let her be clumsy, or let her be slim,
   Young or ancient, I care not a feather;
So fill up a bumper, nay, fill to the brim,
   Let us toast all the ladies together.

Of all your beauties, one by one,
   I pledge, dear, I am thinking;
Before the tale were well begun
   I had been dead of drinking.

They talk about a woman's sphere as though it had
      a limit;
There's not a place on earth or heaven,
There's not a task to mankind given,
There's not a blessing or a woe,
There's not a whispered yes or no,
There's not a life or birth,
That has a feather's weight of worth—
   Without a woman in it.

To woman in her higher, nobler aspects, whether wife, widow, grass widow, mother-in-law, hired girl, telegraph operator, telephone helloer, queen, book agent, wet nurse, stepmother, boss, professional fat woman, professional double-headed woman or professional beauty—God bless her.

—Samuel L. Clemens.

Tween woman and wine a man's lot is to smart,
For wine makes his head ache, and woman his heart.

We've toasted the mother and daughter
We've toasted the sweetheart and wife;
But somehow we missed her,
Our dear little sister—
The joy of another man's life.

What, sir, would the people of the earth be without
woman? They would be scarce, sir, almighty scarce.
                                              —Samuel L. Clemens.

SEE ALSO: *General; Love; Lust; Parents; Wives; Weddings.*

World's Worst Toasts

Over time, the human mind has composed a mind-numbing accumulation of bad toasts. Even the most seemingly narrow category of toast is liable to produce a set of genuine groaners. For instance, take hardware dealing and try to decide which of these is the worst:

To the hardware dealer: Who, if he keeps hammering away on the level, will nail plenty of customers, providing he's on the square. That's plane to see.

or

Here's to the fellow who can stand on his own two feet and face the world squarely without blinking an eye. He calls a spade a spade.

or

To the hardware trade—although they profess to honesty, they sell iron and steel for a living.

Here are fifteen of the author's all-star best of the worst:

A hobo is seen by the side of the road running a lighted

match up and down the seams of his shirt by a passer-by, who asks, "What are you doing?" Hobo: "Toasting the visitors."

A pretzel and un stein o'peer,
And thou, mit sixteen kinder,
Ach, my lieber frau,
Sitting beside me, those garden in—
Ach! dat were baradise already now!

A wee little dog passed a wee little tree.
Said the wee little tree, "Won't you have one on
  me?"
"No" said the little dog, no bigger than a mouse. "I just had one on the house."

Dismay to unskilled surgeons—who, like the nocturnal feline, mew-till-late and destroy patients.

Here's to love, ain't life grand!
Just got a divorce from my old man.
I laughed and laughed at the judge's decision;
He gave him all the kids,
And none of 'em were his'n!

Here's to the Laplanders—cold and haughty: And here's to their southern sisters—not quite so much so.

I feel just like a loaf of bread. Wherever I go—they toast me.

I propose a little toast.
You'll have to do better than that—I'm hungry.

Let us drink a toast to the queer old dean.

—Toast allegedly proposed by the Reverend William A. Spooner to Queen Victoria, his "dear old queen." Spooner, of course, was responsible for innumerable "tips of the slongue."

May the village "belle" never be too long in the clapper!

—Old English.

May those who'd be rude to American roses
Feel a thorn's fatal prick in their lips and their noses.

O Woman! Lovely Woman!
You're just like a gun;
You're loaded up with powder
And wadded most a ton;
You set your cap with care,
And with a "bang" you slyly shoot
Your eyeballs at his stare. Oh Fudge!

To Hay Fever—Here's looking at-chooo!

To the one we love—When she is our toast we don't
want any *but her.*

Woman's hair; beautiful hair,
    What words of praise I'd utter—
But, oh, how sick it makes me feel,
    To find it in the butter.

AULD LANG SYNE (1).

Should auld acquaintance be forgot
   And never brought to mind,
Should auld acquaintance be forgot
   And days o' lang syne.
For auld lang syne, my dear,
   For auld lang syne,
We'll tak' a cup o' kindness yet
   For auld lang syne.

Auld Lang Syne. An old postcard. *(Author's collection)*

ACKNOWLEDGMENTS

I break my bones before you.
                    —Japanese. It refers to the
                    severest form of genuflection.

The idea for this book first came to me during the
summer of 1977 after I had bought, for a nickel, a slim
collection of toasts at a library book sale in Maine. That
collection, which was published in 1908, got me started
as a toast collector, and so my first indebtedness must
go to Idelle Phelps, the author of *Your Health!*

Beyond Ms. Phelps a number of contemporary institutions and individuals have joined my conspiracy to
revive the toast. First, I am obliged to a legion of reference librarians spread geographically from Boston to
San Diego who helped me get a bead on my dusty
quarry. The staffs of the Library of Congress, the
Wayne State University Folklore Archives, and the
Public Library of Cincinnati and Hamilton County
were extraordinarily helpful in this regard.

The Wine Museum of San Francisco (Ernest G. Mit-
telberger and Mary M. Rodgers especially), the United
States Brewer's Association (Chester E. Gardner in particular), the Warshaw Collection of Business
Americana at the Smithsonian Institution (Dr. John N.

Hoffman and Lorene Mayo specifically), and the Genesee County Museum, Mumford, N.Y. (Lara Todorov), provided me with invaluable help. Al Durante, a gentleman with A. Smith Bowman, the company that produces Virginia Gentleman, allowed me access to his fine collection of toasts, as did the aforementioned gent from Dublin, Jack McGowan. I would also like to thank David Wachsman of the Irish Whiskey Information Bureau in New York for his interest in this project and for putting me in touch with Jack McGowan.

I would also like to thank a number of friends (John Masterman, Bob Skole, Joseph C. Goulden, Florenz Baron, Elaine Viets, and Mariquita Mullan) for their contributions, not the least of which was their enthusiasm. Sandra Einbinder typed, corrected, and watched over the final manuscript. Neda Abrams of Guinness and M. K. Paskus, Protocol Officer at the U.S. Department of State, must also be singled out for their help. My mother did her usual fine job as research assistant —in this case coming up with a dozen or so of the book's best toasts. Finally, thanks to Nancy, to whom all the nice toasts under *Love* apply (to say nothing of a few under *Lust*).

Here's to all!

BIBLIOGRAPHY

The cause of Bibliomania all over the world.
    —Toast of the Roxburghe Club, 1812.

"Adept," *Everybody's Toast Book.* Philadelphia and Baltimore: Fisher & Bro., n.d.

Alderson, William A. *Here's To You.* New York: Dodge Publishing Co., 1907.

Allen, Edward Frank. *Modern Humor for Effective Speaking.* New York: Dover Publishing, 1945.

Allen, Steve. *Curses or How Never to be Foiled Again.* Los Angeles: J.P. Tarcher, 1973.

Anderson, Stewart. *Sparks of Laughter.* Newark, N.J.: Stewart Anderson, 1922.

Anderson, Will. *The Beer Book.* Princeton, N.J.: Pyne Press, 1973.

Antrim, Minna Thomas. *A Book of Toasts.* Philadelphia: Henry Altemus Co., 1902.

Aye, John. *The Humor of Drinking.* London: Universal Publishing Co., 1934.

Benham, Sir Gurney. *Benham's Book of Quotations, Proverbs and Household Words.* New York: G. P. Putnam's Sons, 1936.

Bennett, James O'Donnell. *When Good Fellows Get Together.* Chicago: The Reilly & Britton Co., 1908.

Berman, Frederick. *The Complete Toastmaster.* London: Blandford Press, 1953.

Birmingham, Frederick. *Falstaff's Complete Beer Book.* New York: Award Books, 1970.

Blake, Rodney. *After-Dinner Verses.* New York: A.L. Burt Co., n.d.

Book of Good Fellowship, The., (no author, publisher, or date)

Botkin, B.A. *Treasury of American Anecdotes.* New York: Bonanza, n.d.

Braude, Jacob. *Braude's Handbook of Stories for Toastmasters and Speakers.* Englewood Cliffs, N.J.: Prentice-Hall, 1957.

Braude, Jacob. *Complete Speaker's and Toastmaster's Library,* 8 Volumes. Englewood Cliffs, N.J.: Prentice-Hall, 1957.

Bredenbek, Magnus. *What Shall We Drink.* New York: Carlyle House, 1934.

Brooks, Fred Emerson. *Cream Toasts.* Chicago: Forbes and Co., 1915.

Brooks, Fred Emerson. *Patriotic Toasts.* Chicago: Forbes and Co., 1919.

Brown, John Hull. *Early American Beverages.* Rutland, Vt.: Charles E. Tuttle Co., 1966.

Burton, Alexander. *After Dinner Speeches.* 1921.

Butler, Anthony. *The Book of Blarney.* New York: Dell Publishing Co., 1969.

Cahill, F.J. *A Bunch of Yarns.* New York: The Outing Publishing Co., 1906.

Campbell, Andrew. *The Book of Beer.* London: Dennis Dobson, 1956.

Case, Carleton B. *The Big Toast Book.* Chicago: Shrewsbury Publishing, 1927.

Charles (formerly of Delmonico's). *Cheerio!* New York: The Elf, 1930.

Chase, Edithe Lea, and Capt. W.E.P. French. *Maes Hael—The Book of Toasts.* New York: Grafton Press, 1904.

Clode, Edward J. *2088 Jokes, Toasts and Anecdotes.* New York: Grosset and Dunlap, 1921.

Clotho. *Prosit: A Book of Toasts.* San Francisco: Paul Elder & Co., 1908.

Cobb, Irvin S. *Irvin S. Cobb's Own Recipe Book.* Frankfort, Ky.: Frankfort Distilleries, 1934.

Conelly, Bertha, and Helen Ramsey. *Modern Toasts for All Occasions.* Minneapolis, Minn.: Northwestern Press, n.d.

Copeland, Lewis and Faye. *10,000 Jokes, Toasts and Stories.* Garden City, N.Y.: Halcyon House, 1940.

Copeland, Lewis. *Popular Quotations for All Uses.* Garden City, N.Y.: Garden City Publishing Co., 1942.

Crowley, Charles E. *The Perfect Bartending Host at Home.* New York: Huma Publishing Co., 1933.

Davis, Bert. *Crisp Toasts.* New York: H.M. Caldwell Co., 1907.

Davis, Harry Cassell. *Commencement Parts.* New York: Noble and Noble, 1929.

Dodge, W.W. *The Fraternal and Modern Banquet Orator.* Burlington, Iowa: W.W. Dodge, 1903.

Donahue, Harold. *The Toastmaster's Manual.* Indianapolis: Maxwell Drake, 1945.

Douglas, Ronald Macdonald. *The Scots Book.* New York: E.P. Dutton, n.d.

Dwiggins, Clare Victor. *Toast Book.* Philadelphia: John C. Winston Co., 1905.

Edgerton, A.C. *A Speech for Every Occasion.* New York: Noble and Noble, 1949.

Edmund, Peggy, and H.W. Williams. *Toaster's Handbook.* New York: H.W. Wilson & Co., 1914.

Eleven Cellars Wines. *A Book of Wine and Toasts.* Delano, Calif.: Eleven Cellars Wines, n.d.

Emerson, Edward R. *Beverages, Past and Present,* Vol. II. New York: G.P. Putnam's Sons, 1908.

Erdoes, Richard. *Saloons of the Old West.* New York: Knopf, 1979.

Espy, Willard R. *The Life and Works of Mr. Anonymous.* New York: Hawthorne Books, 1977.

Fenno, R.F. *Toasts and Maxims.* New York: Fenno, 1908.

Fleming, Atherton. *Gourmet's Book of Food and Drink.* London: Bodley Head, 1933.

Fougner, G. Selmer. *Along the Wine Trail.* New York: The New York Sun Publishing Co., 1935.

Fowler, Nathaniel. *Witty Stories for All Occasions.* New York: Sully and Co., 1915.

French, Richard Valpy. *Nineteen Centuries of Drink in England.* London: Longmans, Green, and Co., 1884.

French, Richard Valpy. *The History of Toasting or Drinking of Healths in England.* London: National Temperance Publication Depot, n.d.

Friedman, Edward L. *Toastmaster's Treasury.* New York: Harper and Row, 1960.

Fuller, Edmund. *Thesaurus of Epigrams.* New York: Crown Publishers, 1943.

Gayre, G.R., *Wassail! In Mazers of Mead.* London: Phillimore & Co., 1964.

Glover, Ellye Howell. *Dame Curtsey's Book of Novel Entertainments for Every Day in the Year.* Chicago: A.C. McClurg & Co., 1927.

Goodfellow, Adam, and William Payne. *A Book of Old Songs, Healths, Toasts, Sentiments and Wise Sayings Pertaining to the Bond of Good Fellowship.* New York: New Amsterdam Book Co., 1901.

Gray, Arthur. *Toasts and Tributes.* New York: Rhode & Haskins, 1904.

Hackwood, Frederick W. *Inns, Ales, and Drinking Customs of Old England.* London: T. Fisher Unwin, 1909.

Harrison, John. *After-Dinner Stories.* Philadelphia: The Penn Publishing Co., 1910.

Hartman, J.F. *Spice and Parody.* New York: The Outing Publishing Co., 1906.

Harvey, James Clarence. *Over the Nuts and Wine.* Boston: H.M. Caldwell, 1906.

Harwell, Richard Barksdale. *The Mint Julep.* Savannah: The Beehive Press, 1975.

Heath, Ambrose. *Good Drinks.* London: Faber and Faber, 1939.

Henry, Lewis C. *Toasts for All Occasions.* Garden City, N.Y.: Halcyon House, 1949.

Herford, Oliver, and John Cecil Clay. *Happy Days.* New York: Mitchell Kennerley, 1917.

Hewitt, W.C. *The Best After-Dinner Stories and How to Tell Them.* Chicago: Charles T. Powner Co., 1946.

Hughes, T. *The Toastmaster's Guide.* London: Hughes, 1806.

Huston, Marvyn J. *Toasts to the Bride and How to Propose Them.* Rutland, Vt.: Charles Tuttle, 1968.

Iverson, William. *O the Times! O the Manners!* New York: William Morrow & Co., 1965.

Jeffery, Barbara. *Wedding Speeches and Toasts.* Slough, Berks, England: W. Foulsam & Co., 1971.

Jenkins, Dudley. *Toasts and After-Dinner Speeches: How to Respond to Toasts or to Make Other Public Addresses, and Always to Say the Right Thing in the Right Way.* Philadelphia: Penn Publishing Co., 1933.

Kaser, Arthur Leroy. *Good Toasts and Funny Stories.* Chicago: T.S. Denison & Co., Chicago, 1923.

Kaser, Arthur Leroy. *Toasts and Stories for Every Occasion.* Dayton, Ohio: Paine Publishing Co., 1934.

Kearney, Paul W. *Toasts and Anecdotes.* New York: Edward J. Clode, 1923.

Kelly, Joan Larson. *Irish Wit and Wisdom.* Mt. Vernon, N.Y.: Peter Pauper Press, n.d.

Lewis, E.C. *Toasts for All Occasions.* Boston: Mutual Book Co., 1903.

Lewis, E.L. *Everybody Up—A Book of Toasts.* Boston: H.M. Caldwell, 1909.

Loots, Barbara Kunz. *The Little Book of Toasts.* Kansas City: Hallmark, 1975.

Lowe, Paul E. *The 20th-Century Book of Toasts.* Philadelphia: David McKay, 1910.

Lupton, Martha. *The Treasury of Modern Humor.* Indianapolis: Maxwell Droke, 1938.

McClure, John, and William Rose Benet. *The Stag's Hornbook.* New York: Knopf, 1945.

McIvor, Ivor Ben. *Scottish Toasts.* New York: H.M. Caldwell, 1908.

McLean, James Monroe. *The Book of Wine.* Philadelphia: Dorrance and Co., 1934.

Madison, Janet. *Toasts You Ought to Know.* Chicago: Reilly & Britton Co., 1908.

Marchant, W.T. *In Praise of Ale.* London: George Redway, 1888.

Meiers, Mildred, and Jack Knapp. *Thesaurus of Humor.* New York: Crown, 1940.

Monson-Fitzjohn, G.J. *Drinking Vessels of Bygone Days.* London: Herbert Jenkins, 1927.

Morewood, Samuel. *Inventions and Customs of Ancient and Modern Nations in the Manufacture and Use of Inebriating Liquors.* Dublin: 1838.

Morrison, Lillian. *Yours Till Niagara Falls.* New York: Thomas Y. Crowell Co., 1950.

Muller, Helen M. *Still More Toasts.* New York: H.W. Wilson Co., 1932.

Murphy, J.F. *Five Hundred Popular and Up-To-Date Toasts.* Boston: J.F. Murphy, n.d.

Nesbit, Wilbur. *The Loving Cup: Original Toasts by Original Folks.* Chicago: P.F. Volland and Co., 1909.

Nesbit, Wilbur D. *After-Dinner Speeches and How to Make Them.* Chicago: Reilly & Lee Co., 1927.

Noolas, Rab. *Merry Go Down.* East Ardsley, Wakefield, Yorkshire, England: Reproduced by S.R. Publishers, 1971.

Old English Drinking Songs. Cincinnati: Byway Press, n.d.

Owen, Peter. *A History of Gin.* London: 1976.

Phelps, Idelle. *Your Health!* Philadelphia: George W. Jacobs, 1906.

Pittinger, William. *Toasts and Forms of Public Address.* Philadelphia: The Penn Publishing Co., 1900.

Price, E. Cox. *Bons Mots for Menus.* London: Practical Press, 1935.

Prochnow, Herbert V. *The Public Speaker's Treasure Chest.* New York: Harper and Bros., 1942.

Prochnow, Herbert V. *Toastmaster's Handbook.* New York: Prentice-Hall, 1949.

Proskauer, Julien J. *What'll You Have?* New York: A.L. Burt, 1933.

Prynne, William. *Healthes: Sicknesse.* London: 1628.

Pudney, John. *The Harp Book of Toasts.* London: Harp Lager, 1963.

Ramsay, William. *A Book of Toasts.* New York: Dodge Publishing Co., 1906.

Reynolds, Cuyler. *The Banquet Book.* New York: G.P. Putnam, 1902.

Rice, Wallace and Frances. *Toasts and Tipple: A Book of Conviviality.* New York: M.A. Donohue and Co., 1914.

Roach, J. *The Royal Toastmaster.* London: Roach, 1791.

Rodgers, H.A. *Toasts and Cocktails.* St. Louis: Shallcross Printing and Stationary Co., 1905.

Rowe, Col. William H., Jr. *Campaign Verse and Toasts.* Albany: J.B. Lyon and Co., 1908.

Russell, Ralph. *Mix and Be Merry.* Vancouver: J.J. Douglas, 1974.

Sargent, John William, and Nella Fontaine Binckley. *Toasts for the Times in Pictures and Rhymes.* Chicago: Saalfield Publishing Co., 1906.

Schmidt, William. *The Flowing Bowl.* New York: Charles L. Webster, 1892.

"Shane Na Gael," *Irish Toasts.* New York: H.M. Caldwell, 1908.

Shay, Frank. *Drawn From the Wood.* New York: Gold Label Books, 1929.

Simon, Andre L. *Bottlescrew Days: Wine Drinking in England During the Eighteenth Century.* London: Duckworth, 1926.

Simon, Andrew Louis. *Drink.* New York: Horizon Press, 1953.

Speeches and Toasts: How to Make and Propose Them. London: Ward, Lock & Co, n.d.

Stafford, William Young. *Toasts and Speeches.* Chicago: Frederick J. Drake and Co., 1902.

Sullivan, James. *Smart Toasts for the Smart Set.* New York: M.J. Ivers, 1903.

Sutherland, Natalie M. *Toasts, Jokes and Limericks.* Reader Mail, 1937.

Swan, Harry Percival. *Flashes of Wit and Wisdom.* Belfast: The Quota Press, 1952.

Tavern Anecdotes and Reminiscences of the Origin of Signs, Clubs, Coffee-Houses, Streets, City Companies, Wards, & C, By One of the Old School. London: William Cole, 1881.

Thiselton, William Matthew. *National Anecdotes: Interspersed with Historical Facts; English Proverbial Sayings and Maxims with Collection of Toasts and Sentiments,* Vol. III. London: Cradock and Joy, 1812.

Toasts. St. Louis, Mo.: The William J. Lemp Brewing Co., 1896, 1908.

Toasts and After-Dinner Stories. New York: Barse and Hopkins, n.d.

Viets, Elaine. "Here's Mud in Your Eye." St. Louis *Post-Dispatch*, December 26, 1976.

Waters, Margaret. *Toasts.* New York: Barse and Hopkins, 1909.

Watson, Rowland. *Merry Gentlemen.* London: T. Werner Laurie, 1951.

Williams, Victor W. *"Hello Bill" Toasts.* San Francisco: Whitaker & Ray Co., 1903.

Wood, Katharine B. *Quotations for Occasions.* New York: The Century Co., 1896.

Woolard, Sam F. *Good Fellowship.* Wichita, Kans.: Goldsmith Woolard Publishing Co., 1904.

Wright, Richardson. *The Bed-Book of Eating and Drinking*. Philadelphia: J.B. Lippincott, 1943.

AUTHOR INDEX

Gay, John, 103
Goldsmith, Oliver, 159, 193,
    220
Graham, Harry, 263
Guest, Edgar A., 265

Halpine, Charles G., 129
Harte, Bret, 253
Haskins, Henry Stanley, 40
Hassoldt, W.L., 53
Hayez, Jean C., 89
Haynes, W. Knox, 160
Hemingway, Ernest, 213
Herbert, A.P., 256, 284
Herford, Oliver, 66, 84, 120,
    171, 206, 243, 253, 281, 282
Herrick, Robert, 50, 221
Holmes, Oliver Wendell, 35,
    44, 60, 74, 215, 245, 254,
    284
Hood, Thomas, 262
Horace, 282
Hovey, Richard, 97, 279
Howell, James, 281

Hubbard, Elbert, 170
Hugo, Victor, 241
Hunt, Leigh, 94, 153

Irish, 37, 45, 47, 48, 61, 69, 70,
    71, 80, 84, 92, 96, 115, 118,
    119, 130, 131, 136, 137,
    144–50, 166, 186, 187, 188,
    189, 199, 224–5, 277
Irwin, Wallace, 90, 131, 250

Jackson, Andrew, 127
Jarrold, Ernest, 83, 259, 278
Jefferson, Joseph, 103
Jefferson, Thomas, 126
Johnson, Ben, 37, 64, 106, 156
Johnson, Larry E., 36
Johnson, Samuel, 274
Jones, Dean, 74